Guevara

Andrew Sinclair

Fontana/Collins

First published in Fontana 1970
Copyright © Andrew Sinclair 1970
Printed in Great Britain
for the Publishers Wm. Collins Sons & Co. Ltd.,
14 St. James's Place, London, S.W.1,
by Richard Clay (The Chaucer Press), Ltd.,
Bungay, Suffolk

Manas Chitakasem

Modern Masters

Editor Frank Kermode

By Modern Masters we mean the men who
have changed and are changing the life and
thought of our age. Everybody wants to
know who they are and what they say, but
hitherto it has often been very difficult to
find out. This series makes it easy. Each
volume is clear, concise and authoritative.
Nothing else can offer in such an acceptable
form an assured grasp of these revolutionary
thinkers. The authors are themselves
masters, and they have written their books in
the belief that general discussion of their
subjects will henceforth be more informed
and more exciting than ever before.

Frank Kermode

Modern Masters

Contents

In a real sense, this book was only written because of the extensive research and Cuban experience of Marianne Alexandre

1 The Background of a Revolutionary

'I was born in Argentina, I fought in Cuba, and I began to be a revolutionary in Guatemala.' This is what Che Guevara called his autobiographical synthesis. It was also the synthesis of a continent, caught in the contradiction between reactionary governments and utopian revolutions. Guevara, who was the first man since Bolívar with a serious plan to unite the cat-fighting congeries of countries which called themselves Latin America, lived out the thesis and antithesis of his place and time.

Born into a privileged family of Spanish and Irish descent in 1928, Ernesto Guevara de la Serna was to react strongly from his background. Yet his outwardly conventional family, who lived in the little city of Alta Gracia, was in fact exceptionally radical, dynamic and open-minded. Ernesto Guevara, who later received the nickname of Che, did not rebel from his free-thinking home; he rebelled from the oppression of his continent. As Ricardo Rojo, a friend of the family, testifies, certain things were taken for granted in the Guevara household—'a passion for justice, the rejection of fascism, religious indifference, an interest in literature and love of poetry, and a prejudice against money and the ways of making it.' This home conditioning naturally led to a feeling of rebelliousness, which was to make Che into a revolutionary, once he could understand the social problems of South America.

Che acted as if he were a youth as a boy and a man as a youth. A classmate found him 'incredibly sure of himself and totally independent in his opinions ... very dynamic, restless and unconventional.' To a teacher, Che 'looked and acted much older than he was, and was clearly already grown up with a definite personality, moody and undisciplined, but extremely mature.' While he was still at high school, his friends were university students who accepted him as their equal. His realism already outweighed their wish for romantic protest. On one occasion, when asked to take to the streets in a political demonstration, he refused with the cold remarks, 'Go out into the streets so that the police can hit us with their clubs? Nothing doing. I'll go and demonstrate only if you give me a gun.' Such a hard assessment of the situation in his youth makes Che's later assertion plausible, that a man at fifteen already knows what he wants to die for and is not afraid of giving his life if he has found an ideal which makes the sacrifice easy.

By temperament, Che looked on difficulties as challenges. Disabilities were to be defeated, barriers to be broken. A marked trait of Che's personality throughout his life appeared in his early fight against asthma. He became an athlete in spite of terrible asthma attacks which forced him to run off the rugby field to inhale his medicine. He became a hardened traveller who merely halted whenever he could not breathe and went on when he could. He got through a six-years' course in three years at university, passing sixteen major examinations in six months in spite of forty-five serious asthma attacks. His aunt said of this time, 'We would listen to him gasping, studying as he lay on the floor to ease his breathing, but he never complained. For him, it was a challenge.' By the greatest irony of all, a board of army doctors declared him unfit for any sort of military service, once he had reached the age of eighteen. His military training had to wait a while.

His grandmother's death from cancer and his mother's struggle against the same disease influenced Che to become a doctor. He wanted to try to find a cure for this disease. He would not accept even a family tragedy. He could not see pain and death without wanting to strike at the root cause of it all. When later he was to see that pain and misery were curable, he was again to try and strike at the root cause of it all. He had no resignation in him. He could not stand the passive acceptance of suffering. His nature was to challenge, even the impossible.

In 1946 the Guevara family moved to Buenos Aires, where Che started his medical studies. He was a sporadic student, preferring to overwork at the last moment, and to travel the rest of the time. A friend and travelling companion, Alberto Granados, noticed that Che was not interested in getting good marks, but in studying only what concerned him. And his concern was chiefly for the beauties of the South American landscape and the miseries of its population. After touring Argentina on a bicycle and signing on as a sailor for a trip to the Caribbean, Che finally set off with Granados for a hobo's tour of the whole continent. The pair worked as truck-drivers, porters, doctors and dishwashers; at one time, Che was even a guard for a North American mining company in Chile. But the most telling job of the two Argentines was when they worked in a leper colony at San Pablo on the Amazon; there Che saw that the highest kinds of human solidarity and loyalty were formed among lonely and desperate men. Che ended the trip starving in Miami, but he somehow got back to Buenos Aires to complete his work for his medical degree.

This grand tour at subsistence level was the evidence and basis for Che's feeling that he knew the Americans and their problems. He stated later that he had never felt like a foreigner anywhere. 'I felt Guatemalan in Guatemala, Mexican in Mexico, Peruvian in Peru.' The journey also began to change him from a doctor into a radical. In a speech in 1960, he remembered the beginnings of this change. 'Because of the conditions in which I travelled, I came into close contact with poverty and hunger and disease. I discovered that I was unable to cure sick children through lack of means, and I saw the degradation of under-nourishment and constant repression. In this way, I began to realize that there was another thing which was as important as being a famous researcher or making a great contribution to medical science: and that was to help those people.'

The rough conditions of travel had another effect. They proved to Che that he could endure great hardship and privation—that existence in the margins of survival necessary to any guerrilla fighter. His friends noticed that he could live in the most sinister places and still keep his sense of humour. He only tolerated a travelling companion who could walk huge distances, forget about clothing and go without money. He could also manage to keep going, even when he had not eaten for three days. The fact of being poor among the poor made Che feel their indignation against their exploiters, their comradeship among themselves, and led him to the self-discipline which he needed to become their leader.

Two months after Che had qualified as a doctor in 1953 with a thesis on allergies, he threw away his career—to his father's annoyance. He left Argentina for Bolivia, which was being ruled by the first effective reform government in its history. The new régime nationalized the country's tin mines, which were perhaps the largest and the worst-run in the world, and it distributed the waste of the barren *altiplano* among the Indians, who had held no claim to their own lands since their conquest by the Spanish in the 16th century. Che was not yet a Marxist nor a revolutionary; according to his friend Rojo, his chief interest was still medicine and archaeology, not politics. Yet this first-hand contact with a large programme of social change in action turned Che towards the ideas of revolutionary progress. Paradoxically enough, Bolivia seems to have been the country which both inspired Che's political career and killed him.

Che already knew that the Bolivian revolution of 1953 was probably doomed to partial failure. He and Rojo interviewed the Minister for Peasant Affairs and were disappointed by him. Standing later in the street in front of a statue of Bolívar, Che said: 'The question is one of fighting the causes and not just being satisfied with getting rid of the effects. This revolution is bound to fail if it doesn't manage to break down the spiritual isolation of the Indians, if it doesn't succeed in reaching deep inside them, stirring them right down to the bone, and giving them back their stature as human beings. Otherwise, what's the use?'

The two friends also visited the great mines of Siglo XX. and Catavi. The Minister of Mines, Juan Lechín, had claimed that the revolution was more deep-rooted in Bolivia than even in China. But Che remained unconvinced. The fact that the government had raised the wages of the miners when it had nationalized the mines made Che gloomy. He thought that it was a grave error to confuse the necessities of a nation in arms with the bribes paid to workers when a business changed hands. For a pittance, the miners had lessened the material and moral reserves of a revolution that would need every reserve it had in the end. None of Che's friends in Bolivia could change his mind.

Che and Rojo left Bolivia by truck with a party of Indians, heading for Peru. Rojo's account of the Indians' reactions to himself and Che is a prophecy of the reactions that Che would meet as a guerrilla in Bolivia fifteen years later.

The trip was an indispensable one in our education about the America of the Indians. We entered a hostile world, we were trapped between bundles and people who looked like bundles. There was silence. Jolts, bruises and silence. We found out that it was impossible to try and show our sympathy before those eyes of metal which stared at us, those lips as tight and forbidding as a

> *vice that refused to reply to our questions ... We couldn't communicate in any human way with the Indians, yet the guards at the Peruvian border were absolutely convinced that we had turned their heads with ideas about agrarian revolution.*

With other Argentine students, Che and Rojo travelled on to tropical Guayaquil. There Che made a decision that he never revoked. He had sworn to join his friend Granados at the leper colony at San Pablo, but he needed little persuasion by the Argentine students to continue on with them to Guatemala, where there was another revolution in action, which might set a pattern for the change of the continent. As Rojo says, Che was not yet a Marxist, and was not yet really interested in politics. But another friend noticed that Che already seemed to be feel responsible for all the world's injustices. He was groping his way towards the root cause of all the misery he had seen and sometimes shared among the poor of Latin America. But he was still unread in political philosophy. He saw the evidence of exploitation, but not the method of changing the system.

Juan Bosch, who later became a short-term and reforming President of the Dominican Republic, also met Che at this time. He found that Che 'was intensely preoccupied with what he saw. He seemed dissatisfied with all solutions proposed up to that time, and when he was asked specific questions, he criticized all parties, but he never defined his own position.' Yet Bosch was convinced by the way that Che answered questions that Che had not yet become a Communist. His heart was moving before his mind. His sense of liberty was still in conflict with his feeling that a bureaucracy might have to run a socialist state. He needed to see another revolution in being and to study revolutionary thought, in order to find a system for change.

Jacobo Arbenz, who led the new revolutionary government in Guatemala, had a lasting influence on Che. Backed by a coalition of young army officers and intellectuals, Arbenz had decided to tackle the most dangerous reform of all. When Che arrived in 1953, Arbenz was redistributing to the Indians and the peasants large areas of the land just nationalized from the United Fruit Company. The danger of the reform lay in provoking a counterattack by large interests in the United States, for the United Fruit Company had long been used to controlling what it called 'banana republics' for the benefit of its American shareholders. Arbenz not only brought Che up against the realities of North American economic power. He also defined the political character of his régime in terms that were not materialist. 'Man is not just a stomach,' Arbenz declared, 'We believe that, above all, he hungers for dignity.' This attitude was central in Che's later thinking, which elaborated this same concept of the socialist who is not and cannot be a materialist in outlook, because true socialism is a negation of materialism. Throughout his life, Che remained an admirer of Arbenz and his programme.

Yet Che's admiration was not enough. His wish to work for the revolution as a doctor in the jungles of the Peten fell foul of his distrust of bureaucracy. He visited the minister in charge of the Public Health Department and seemed to be accepted, until he was asked for his card. 'What card?' Guevara answered. The minister replied that naturally Che had to be a member of the Guatemalan Labour Party, another name for the local Communist Party. Che replied that he was a revolutionary and did not believe that affiliations of that sort meant anything. Anyway, he would never join the Party from a sense of obligation, only from a sense of conviction. He did not get the job.

The downfall of the Arbenz régime in 1954 was Che's baptism in the practical techniques of revolution and counterrevolution. In retaliation for the seizure of the plantations of the United Fruit Company, the Eisenhower government had permitted the Central Intelligence Agency to begin organizing and financing a *coup d'état* in Guatemala. Three factors were working in favour of the CIA plot. First, the Guatemalan army officers behind Arbenz were becoming discouraged by the slow pace of the revolution, which had not yet had the time to win the support and confidence of the Indian masses in Guatemala. Secondly, the régime itself was split by personal ambitions which hid themselves in ideological differences. Thirdly, the middle classes were becoming frightened by the government's open defiance of the United States.

By the end of January 1954, Arbenz was accusing the Eisenhower administration of organizing an invasion of Guatemala by exiles. This accusation, however, did not unite the country behind Arbenz. It merely accentuated the divisions in his own party and the fears of the Guatemalans. On June 18, Guatemala was invaded by the troops of Castillo Armas, trained by the CIA and well-equipped. The Guatemalan army refused to arm the people, for fear of losing its own position of power. The Arbenz régime fell apart in bickering and recriminations.

This collapse brought out the activist in Che. For the first time, he joined in the resistance. He rushed from one small group of young revolutionaries to another, trying to get them to combine and take over Guatemala City. He had a strategy and plan of defence, but he could not find any group to adopt it. He encouraged the Guatemalans as much as he could, urged them to fight for their revolution, transported weapons from place to place. But he did nothing of any use. As the Argentine ambassador told him, he could not do by himself what the government was not willing to do. When Arbenz weakly resigned and Armas took over, Che had to flee for asylum to the Argentine embassy, as he had already been marked for execution by right-wing groups in Guatemala. There he stayed as a virtual prisoner for almost two months, analysing the failure of the revolution.

Régis Debray was to write later, 'For a revolutionary, failure is a springboard. As a source of theory it is richer than victory: it accumulates experience and knowledge.' Che may have been futile in his attempts at action in Guatemala, but he had tried to act. He described himself at the time as being defeated, yet united in his pain to all the Guatemalans, while 'seeking a way to recreate a future for that bleeding land.' Like Antaeus, Che's downfall led him to rise again even more strong; a defeat merely meant more preparation for the victory next time. Above all, it meant more faith in the people, whom Arbenz had not trusted enough to arm or integrate into the political structure of the country.

If the CIA had won a temporary victory for North American financial interests in Guatemala, it had also conjured up a deadly enemy. The naked overthrow of a socialist country by a capitalist plot pushed Che into the study of Marx and Lenin. All the personal hatred that Che felt for the enemies of Arbenz, the subverters of his government and his land reform, seemed to be demonstrated in the explanation of the past and the present history of the world found in the Marxist version of methods of imperialism. A poor and exploited country with a government that was trying to improve the lot of the masses had been deliberately attacked by a rich capitalist power that depended for its dividends on the exploitation of that poor country. It was a text-book example of the worst form of imperialism in practice. For Che Guevara, the United States became the villain of his personal experience and his new ideology. Che's first wife Hilda Gadea wrote, 'It was Guatemala which finally convinced him of the necessity for armed struggle and for taking the initiative against imperialism. By the time he left, he was sure of this.'

Che left for Mexico to study theories of revolution. In Mexico City, where he lived on the margins of existence as poorly as a sparrow in winter, he read the complete works of Marx and Lenin 'and a whole pantheon of Marxist thinkers.' He particularly studied the books dealing with the military strategy in the Spanish Civil War. For many of the refugees from that war had been given asylum in Mexico City, so open in welcoming the losers of foreign battles and so niggardly in feeding them. Under the pressure of hunger and study and experience, Che became a committed radical. The slow progress of social reform in Mexico, still limping forward after many decades of revolutionary rule, did not impress him. 'The Mexican revolution is dead,' he declared. 'It has been dead a long time and we hadn't even noticed.'

This new and fierce radicalism of Che made him ready for his meeting with Fidel Castro in the summer of 1955. Castro had been jailed and exiled from Cuba for leading a failed *coup* against the dictator, Fulgencio Batista. He was looking for a dedicated group of revolutionaries to try an invasion of his country in a second attempt to overthrow Batista. On the night of his first meeting with Fidel Castro, Che joined the Cuban expedition. He was the second to join after Fidel's brother, Raúl. 'It would have taken very little to persuade me,' Che wrote later, 'to join any revolution against a tyranny.' The price was his first marriage. 'I lost my husband,' Hilda Gadea said, 'to the Cuban revolution.'

When Fidel Castro came to pay his last tribute to Che Guevara, he recorded the first meeting between them in terms which owed much to their later conclusions. For in 1955 both men were still romantic and amateur revolutionaries, not revolutionary rulers and experts. But later, Fidel wrote of Che:

He was filled with a profound spirit of hatred and loathing for imperialism, not only because his political awareness was already considerably developed, but also because shortly before, he had had the opportunity of witnessing the criminal imperialist intervention in Guate-

mala through the mercenaries who aborted the revolution in that country. A man like Che did not require elaborate arguments. It was enough for him to know that there were men determined to struggle against that situation, arms in hand; it was enough for him to know that those men were inspired by genuinely revolutionary and patriotic ideals. That was more than enough.

This was the background of a revolutionary. First, a family that felt itself cut off from other privileged families by its consciousness of social inequalities. Then a personal temperament that was intelligent, mature, rebellious and stubborn. Then a wandering over a continent where successions of bad governments had made mass poverty stink in the nostrils and shame the eyes. Then a doctor's concern for curing the incurable millions, whose diseases were only their symptoms, since the root cause was social injustice. Then a personal experience of three failed revolutions—the Bolivian revolution, later to be overthrown by an army *putsch*; the Guatemalan revolution, destroyed by an imperialist intervention; and the Mexican revolution, rotted by internal sloth and decay. This experience changed a young doctor, whose nature was radical, into a revolutionary by intent. He had moved from passive indignation to active resistance, from observing to planning. His sympathy for suffering humanity had become a strategy for finding the remedy for that suffering. To become a total revolutionary, all Che needed was another revolution.

2 The Cuban Revolutionary War

The expedition mounted by Fidel Castro to overthrow Batista in Cuba was nearly certain to fail. The eighty-two men aboard the yacht *Granma* were badly trained, badly equipped and bad sailors. Nobody could navigate the boat properly, everybody was sea-sick, most of the supplies were jettisoned in a storm and the expedition landed in the wrong place at Belic, near the Sierra Maestra, a series of mountain chains in south-east Cuba. The amateurishness of Fidel and Che and the rest of the group in the first weeks of their guerrilla venture could almost have served as a manual of what not to do, just as Che's later book *Guerrilla Warfare* serves as a manual of what to do. Yet the early mistakes of guerrillas are often the lessons for their later successes. All strategists of guerrilla warfare including Che stress the same point, that the initial period is the most dangerous one, and that a few mistakes and bad luck can annihilate the whole group at the outset.

Fidel Castro's force should have been destroyed at the first battle at Alegría de Pío on December 5, 1956. A succession of fatal errors had led them into disaster. One of the few survivors, Universo Sanchez, tells of how his feet were blistered by his new boots, of how their resting-place at Alegría de Pío was exposed to attack, of how they had allowed their guide to leave them and betray them to the nearby troops of Batista, of how ten aeroplanes circled overhead without the guerrillas thinking that the planes were particularly important, and of how they were resting with their weapons laid aside and their boots off. Batista's troops, far more professional than these amateur fighters, surrounded them and nearly wiped them out. The original group was reduced to some twelve men.

In his *Reminiscences of the Cuban Revolutionary War*, which he wrote from notes taken during the campaign, Che describes his experiences with a great deal of irony, modesty and self-criticism. He found the early mistakes of the guerrillas 'both ridiculous and tragic.' He was wounded himself at Alegría de Pío, and his reaction was touching and unsoldierly. ·Not unreasonably, he thought that he was dead, even though the wound did not turn out to be serious. His first concern was not to save his life—the primary duty of a guerrilla—but to die honourably :

> *I immediately began to wonder what would be the best way to die, now that all seemed to be lost. I remembered an old story of Jack London's in which the hero, knowing that he is condemned to freeze to death in the icy wastes of Alaska, leans against a tree and decides to end his life with dignity. This is the only image I remember.*

Che's meditation on American literature was cut short by the curses of Juan Almeida, who forced him to run for his life. Later, Che was to be captured in Bolivia leaning against a tree; but that time, he was wounded in the legs and unable to move, and he was firing until the gun was shot out of his hands.

When Che fled with four of his surviving comrades he made one important and symbolic choice between his duty as a doctor and as a revolutionary. 'This was perhaps the first time I was faced with the dilemma of chosing between my dedication to medicine and my duty as a revolutionary soldier. At my feet were a pack full of medicines and a cartridge box; together, they were tóo heavy to carry. I chose the cartridge box, leaving behind the medicine pack.' Che had learned his first lessons as a guerrilla, that bullets matter more to a guerrilla's survival than even healing.

But he was to make more mistakes. Che found himself

with four other comrades, groping his way towards the Sierra Maestra and a meeting-place with other survivors. Drawing on his recollections of astronomy, he guided the group by the north star. Months later, he discovered that he had even mistaken the north star for another star, and that their arrival in the right place was a matter of sheer luck. Afterwards, Che always carried a compass in his knapsack.

Surrounded by enemy patrols and starving, the five men were totally dependent on help from the peasants of the Sierra Maestra. They were not disappointed. In one peasant's hut they were feasted royally, and a constant procession of neighbours brought them gifts and sympathy. This early reception was to be cold comfort to Che in his last campaign in Bolivia, where after eight-and-a-half months of guerrilla activity, he could write of the Indian peasants there: 'They have to be hunted down to be made to talk, as they are just like little animals.' Certainly without the help of the Cuban peasants, Che's little group would have been exterminated.

Yet the catalogue of early mistakes was not yet complete. Che's group decided to leave their eight guns, all their ammunition and their uniforms in the friendly peasant's hut, along with their one sick comrade 'as security.' They hoped to rejoin Fidel Castro more easily in the disguise of countrymen. But their host betrayed them, not from intention, but from the peasant love of gossiping. Batista's men raided the hut, captured the sick man and seized all the weapons and supplies. When Che's group was led by the peasants to Fidel, their leader castigated their incompetence. Che recorded:

> *For the duration of the campaign and even to-day, his words remain engraved on my mind: 'You have not paid for the error you committed, because the price you pay for the abandonment of your weapons under such cir-*

cumstances is your life. The one and only hope of survival that you would have had, in the event of a frontal clash with the Army, was your guns. To abandon them was criminal and stupid.'

Later, when Che was too ill to keep with the group, he was also left in the care of a friendly peasant; but this time, he was left near the peasant's house without the peasant's wife even knowing that Che was there. Che had become more cautious.

In the case of the few survivors of Alegría de Pío, survival was all. Five peasants joined them in the next month, and early in 1957 they made a successful attack on the La Plata barracks. Most of the rural population was still sitting on the fence and communications with potential rebels in the cities did not exist; but at least, a beginning had been made. As Fidel declared, they now had twelve rifles and a victory to their credit, instead of only seven rifles and no victory at all. Even so, Che's mistakes continued. With rare vanity, he took to wearing a captured corporal's cap as a trophy from the victory. Then one day, the cap was nearly shot from his head while he was out inspecting his own sentries, who naturally took him for an enemy.

The nucleus of the guerrilla force became acclimatized to life in the Sierra Maestra during the following months. There was one traitor among them, but the local population shielded them, although few joined them. As Che was to find later in Bolivia, the hardest thing was to get new recruits. 'In that period, it was very difficult to enlarge our group; a few men came, but others left; the physical conditions of the struggle were very hard, but the problems of morale even more so.' This experience led Che to stress in *Guerrilla Warfare* how important it was never to risk nor waste lives in the early stages, because they were literally irreplaceable.

The months in the Sierra Maestra taught the guerrillas

their dependence on peasant support. The few peasants who actually did join them were vital. They could always get food from their friends among the other peasants, they could pick the rural grapevine for news of enemy movements, and they could teach urban recruits how to survive in the countryside. They were the real scouts and spies and foragers of the group. They helped to form a regional network of sympathizers, who could bring new recruits to the guerrilla band. As the successes and the legend of the 'bearded ones' grew, so peasant support grew. Castro began to establish a kind of extra-legal revolutionary state in a few villages, which also served as warning signals against an army attack.

Peasant support was based as much on calculation as idealism. Che's memoirs of the Cuban war are full of accounts of executions of peasant informers, denounced by other peasants. The rebel force would protect its friends and neutrals and treat them fairly, but it was ruthless towards anyone who helped Batista's men. In many areas of the Sierra Maestra, it was eventually more dangerous to help the government than to help the rebels, unlike in the later war in Bolivia, where Che was perpetually betrayed by peasants whom he could not control nor terrorize into silence. In the Cuban War, however, Che noted of the peasants: 'Denouncing us did violence to their own conscience and, in any case, put them in danger, since revolutionary justice was speedy.'

The role of the peasant in the insurrection was basic to the success of the Castro group and to its understanding of revolutionary philosophy. Che has described the guerrillas' increasing awareness of the peasant's importance:

We began to grow more conscious of the necessity for a definitive change in the life of the people. The idea of agrarian reform became clear and unity with the people ceased to be theory and was converted into a basic ele-

ment of our being. The guerrilla group and the peasantry began to merge into one single mass, without knowing the moment on the long revolutionary road when this happened or when the words became true and we were part of the peasants. As for me, my attempts to treat their illnesses in the Sierra converted my spontaneous and rather lyrical feelings into a force that was worth more and sounder based. Those suffering and loyal inhabitants of the Sierra Maestra have never suspected the role they played in forging our revolutionary ideology.

Such contact with the peasants profoundly affected Che's whole theory of revolutionary strategy. Direct and personal experience in the Sierra Maestra made him begin his work on *Guerrilla Warfare* with three fundamental statements, one of which is that: 'In the underdeveloped countries of the Americas, rural areas are the best battlefields for revolution.' Moreover, he insists that 'the guerrilla makes agrarian reform his banner.' Che and his fellow Cuban revolutionaries emphasized later that they were not indebted to Mao's theories on peasant warfare, stressing that they had not even read his writings nor others of the same kind. Direct experience was always Che's best teacher.

One other lesson was learned in the early days of the war. Castro insisted on his troops behaving as humanely as possible towards wounded enemy soldiers, prisoners, civilians and peasants who did not collaborate with the enemy. The result was that the reputation of the guerrillas grew in contrast to the general brutalities practised by Batista's men. This was of practical help to Che himself, who suffered from a bad bout of asthma. On one occasion, his physical incapacity nearly got the whole Castro group liquidated. In the end, he had to be left behind to recover in the care of peasants, who were won over by the humane policy of the guerrillas. When Che tried to rejoin the group, he was so ill that he had to use his rifle as a crutch and he took ten days to cross ground that he normally crossed in one.

Batista's cruelty in putting down a student plot in Havana brought new and essential help to the thirty men of the guerrilla force. A campaign of terror by the army in the Sierra Maestra had begun to shake the sympathy of the peasants; but now fifty new recruits from the cities joined the guerrillas. Thirty of them were armed, and in May, 1957, a cargo of weapons was delivered to Castro's forces, including machine-guns, automatic rifles, carbines and six thousand rounds of ammunition. Che and the veteran rebels were ecstatic at this accession of strength, although disappointed at the poor quality of the new recruits.

> After a few months of living in the Sierra, we had become veterans, and we saw in the new troops all the defects which those who had landed on the Granma had once had, lack of discipline, inability to adjust to setbacks, indecisiveness, incapacity to adapt to the new life ... the enormous difference between the two groups was easily noticed: ours was disciplined, compact, used to warfare: the newcomers' group was still suffering from the sickness of the first days: they were not used to eating only once a day, and if the rations did not taste good, they would not eat at all. The newcomers had their packs full of useless items, and if the packs were too heavy, they would rather, for example, give up a can of condensed milk than a towel—a crime of lèse guerrilla. We took advantage of this by collecting all the cans of food they left behind.

Yet soon the new recruits distinguished themselves in the battle of El Uvero, in which Che himself played a major part. The 'nomadic phase' discussed by Che in *Guerrilla Warfare* was nearly over. The growth of strength of the guerrilla forces made a vast difference to the attitude of Batista's army as well as to the morale of the guerrillas themselves. As Che noticed: 'There was a qualitative change. There was now a whole area which our enemies avoided for fear of meeting us, although we also showed little interest in bumping into them.'

The 'nomadic phase' of the guerrillas in the Sierra Maestra had been a matter of kill or cure. Extremely incompetent at the beginning, the few survivors of Alegría de Pío soon became seasoned fighters. Partially disabled through ill-health, Che never stopped his analysis of his own and the group's mistakes. Most of his later guerrilla theory—the setting up of a guerrilla focus, survival at all costs in the early days, the concentration on morale—was the direct outcome of his observations. Above all, he learned to appreciate the aid of the peasants, both as recruits and as suppliers for the guerrillas. Although the new recruits and the arms sent from the cities were equally vital, their help in the development of the guerrilla forces was later to be underestimated by Che for political reasons.

The triumph of El Uvero, when guerrillas successfully overwhelmed a small barracks in broad daylight by frontal assault, marked a change in the war. Batista's army withdrew from its outposts in the Sierra Maestra, leaving a large area to the rebels. From this time onwards, Che recalled, the enemy 'made only sporadic incursions into the Sierra ... There was a true liberated zone. Precautionary measures were not so necessary. We were partially free to talk at night, to stir in our hammocks. Authorization was given to move into the Sierra villages and establish a closer relationship with the people.'

But success breeds nearly as many problems as failure. The guerrilla forces had begun a period of continuous growth, which created new problems of food and supplies. The second phase of the guerrilla war had started, with the guerrillas settled in semi-permanent encampments. There, they set up service and supply sections, and became a government in miniature. Small industries, radio stations and hospitals were established, laws were decreed, justice was administered through courts, and an intensive campaign of indoctrination set in motion. The state of armed truce with the Batista army even allowed the guerrillas to make deals with the peasants and village storekeepers for certain crops and supplies. The rebel forces had, for all intents and purposes, converted themselves into something approaching a regular army bivouacking in friendly territory.

Much of the credit for this organization must go to Che. His new-found planning skills date from this period. After the battle of El Uvero, he had been made a Major or *commandante*, the highest rank in the rebel forces, in charge of the Second Column, thus ranking directly beneath Castro himself. Batista's radio stations began to denounce him personally, along with the two Castro brothers. The journalist Enrique Meneses, who spent four months in the Sierra Maestra from December, 1958, testified to Che's success in setting up a supply base for the guerrillas. When he reached Che's camp, he found a hospital housing twenty wounded men and two doctors; an armaments workshop; a tailor's shop making uniforms from olive-green cloth sent from Havana; a bakery; and a printing machine which produced a regular news-sheet. To Meneses, the contrast between Fidel Castro and Che was evident. Fidel was the utopian dreamer, the speech-maker, always on the move, always planning. Che was the silent listener, who wanted a safe base for operations, the pragmatist who could carry out Fidel's dreams. Fidel and Che were interdependent, but already there were those who felt as much loyalty and admiration for Che as for their Cuban chief.

Yet this period of Che's life was not wholly devoted to the actions of the moment. Che was preoccupied not only with winning the war on hand, but with the general principles of all wars of liberation and with the new society to come to Cuba, once victory was won. A comrade, Rafael

Chao, testifies of Che at the time: 'He could be seen, sometimes very late, sitting on his hammock and writing down his notes. He never took a rest without writing down some notes. He also liked discussion very much. When everybody was already asleep, he would take a walk through camp, looking for someone who felt like having a talk.' He used to exchange letters with Raúl Castro, who still disagreed with many of the tenets of Marxism held by Che. And Che himself found that his growing clarity of vision helped his morale, and that of all the guerrillas whom he influenced. 'Our leaders' and fighters' awareness was growing. The best among us felt deeply the need for an agrarian reform and an overturning of the social system, without which the country could never achieve health.'

Throughout *Reminiscences of the Cuban Revolutionary War*, Che's reflective and analytical mind can be seen at work. Most of the ideas contained in his later ideological writings are already nascent. His strategic concepts were certainly born during the Sierra struggle and are contained in the narrative of his combat experience. For instance, he describes the placing of the ambush at El Hombrito and concludes:

> *This battle showed us how easy it was, given certain circumstances, to attack columns on the march. Again, we saw how correct the tactic was of always aiming at the head of the marching troops, in an attempt to kill the first man or the first few men and thus immobilize the whole enemy force. Little by little, we perfected this tactic and finally we made it into such a system that the enemy stopped coming into the Sierra Maestra and their soldiers refused to march in the advance guard.*

He tells of a *post mortem* after another battle, which showed enormous shortcomings, due to a failure to exploit the element of surprise. Che was never content to describe a combat; he had to draw a lesson from it. In fact, the two factors described above, the ambush and the surprise attack, became the basis of his military thinking in *Guerrilla Warfare* and of his actual strategy in his Bolivian campaign.

Fidel Castro had liased with all the opposition parties in Cuba, promising them much in order to get their support against Batista. He had laid great hopes on a general strike, which was called in the cities in April, 1958. But the failure of this general strike proved more than a theoretical setback. It demoralized the opponents of Batista, cut off the lines of supply and communication between the cities and the Sierra Maestra and led to an offensive by Batista's armies which aimed at wiping out the guerrillas during the summer. Che's lack of faith in urban action to support the guerrilla war can be traced back to this failure in the Cuban campaign. He never had much belief in the power of urban revolutionaries, whom he usually considered as soft and unrealistic. And his own 'long march' through the island at the end of Castro's winning campaign in the autumn of 1958, which cut the island in two, confirmed his prejudices against the value of urban action. For he liberated towns from the mountains. He cut off communications between the cities, and thus isolated and finally seized Santa Clara. His own experience was of setting up a rural base, of expanding until towns fell into his hands, of isolating cities until they also fell. To Che, the country had to liberate the city. Urban centres had to be conquered from without, not within. The Sierra campaign and the standpat attitude of the Cuban Communist Party gave Che a strong bias against the Marxist–Leninist dogma of a rising led by the urban proletariat through a series of strikes, through sabotage and through a final revolt. The armed peasants would conquer the countryside until the cities tumbled like rotten bananas into their laps. This was the experience which was to lead Che into geographical isolation in Bolivia.

It is legitimate to spend time on Che's early mistakes and

successes as a guerrilla in the Sierra Maestra. For these twenty-five months of his life made him into an organizer, a thinker, a tactical expert, and something of a hero. He had been merely a young, asthmatic and quixotic urban intellectual, who considered himself a revolutionary because of travel among the Latin American poor and a study of Marx and Lenin. He had been in no way different from thousands of other progressive middle-class Latin Americans in the liberal professions. But by the time that Fidel Castro's provisional government took over from Batista in January, 1959, Che was proved to be a guerrilla fighter of great courage, power and ability. He was now one of the most important men in the new Cuba, and he would soon be looked upon as the most important theorist of the revolution. His job was to put together 'in a systematic and coherent fashion' an ideology from the multitude of contradictory theories proliferating in Cuba in the wake of Castro's victory.

The Cuban War forged Che politically and ideologically. His contact with the peasants turned him into an 'agrarian revolutionary.' The near unanimity of the opposition to Batista's tyranny in the later stages of the struggle made him think in terms of a 'people's war.' The part played by the United States, which aided and supported Batista during most of the war, confirmed Che's hatred of 'Yankee imperialism.' The murky and opportunistic conduct of the politicians opposed to Batista, who allied themselves with Fidel Castro only for their own advantage, disgusted Che with the democratic procedure which threw up such coward connivers. Above all, the actual experience of beginning a war of liberation with a small group, which never grew even as large as one army division, gave Che a set of unorthodox and non-Marxist ideas about guerrilla groups as the new 'flag-bearers' of the revolution. Success depended also, in Che's opinion, on the unquestioned leadership of a chief or *jefe maximo*, who was more important than a whole party organization of anonymous cadres. Publicity, indeed, was a condition of success for the small guerrilla group; fame rallied malcontents to the rebel's side.

From his own experience of guerrilla warfare in Cuba, Che applied maxims to cover most of military strategy and the possibility of world revolution. Three of the recurrent themes in *Reminiscences of the Cuban Revolutionary War* are the basis for all his future thinking.

1. Actual combat is the best way of learning to be a guerrilla fighter. No amount of theory can make a good fighter. Only the experience of a revolutionary war itself can sort out the true *guerrillero* from the dreamer or latent traitor.

2. Actual combat forges an ideologist as well as a fighter. A man may join the guerrilla group, totally ignorant of ideology. But he cannot survive without learning some ideology. His social conscience as a revolutionary must develop hand in hand with his military skill, as military skill alone will never carry him through the hardships of a guerrilla war. Logically, therefore, the best fighter is also the most political man, and he is more fit than anyone else to become a leader after the war is won. For he is more realistic and revolutionary than anyone who has not fought.

3. The guerrilla group has its own mystique. Che's daily contact in the Sierra Maestra with a group of tough, courageous and idealistic men gave him a heroic concept of the *guerrillero*. The pages of his *Reminiscences* are full of tributes to the comrades he lost in the war. Che helped to create this legend of the guerrilla hero, even though this ran against his ideas about equality. And when he himself was to die, he was to incarnate his own legend.

3 Theories of Guerrilla Warfare

Military experts, such as Captain Liddell Hart, may disagree with the political premises which motivated Che Guevara, but they agree that his theories on guerrilla warfare are brilliant strategical studies. Che's writings on the subject have been truly revolutionary. They outline how a rising by a few men may win against the forces of modern armies and technology. Minimal resources, little initial popular support and poor communications are no reason not to begin an insurrection, which can pin down a regular army while gaining new recruits every day. Atom bombs are little use in putting down jungle guerrillas; tanks cannot operate in forests and mountains. The success of the Cuban attempt has inflamed many others; its influence is global. From Vietnam to the Congo, from Nicaragua to Brazil, Che's theories on guerrilla warfare have caught the popular imagination and have held or defeated modern armies, which are equipped to crush anything except this form of fighting. Due to differing political and social factors as well as to military strategy, the guerrillas have succeeded in such places as Algeria and Vietnam, failed in Malaya and Peru and Bolivia, and fought a stalemate in Guatemala, Colombia, Venezuela and the Philippines. Yet none of these wars would have been the same without the influence of Che Guevara.

Che begins his book on *Guerrilla Warfare*, written in 1960, with a famous statement, that the Cuban Revolution 'has proved the people's ability to free themselves from an oppressive government through guerrilla warfare.' He continues to say:

1. Popular forces can win a war against an army.

2. It is not always necessary to have to wait for a revolutionary situation to arise; this can be created by a revolutionary focus.

3. In the underdeveloped countries of the Americas, rural areas are the best battlefields for armed stuggle.

These beliefs allow Che to draw conclusions which refute the policies of the official Communist Parties of Latin America. If popular forces can win a war against an army, then there is nothing to be said for 'the do-nothing attitude of those pseudo-revolutionaries' who say that an army cannot be defeated from without. And if a revolutionary situation can be created, then there is no need to wait until all the required conditions for a theoretical Marxist revolution are ripe. If also guerrillas can be successful in the countryside, then there is no need to wait until urban and industrial groups can take the cities—notoriously prone to a successful counterattack by a regular army.

Yet Che does not deny that the small rural guerrilla force can only operate on one condition. It has to act as the armed advance party of the masses, and thus it has to have popular support. This is an absolute condition. With popular support, the guerrilla force is not numerically inferior to the army, but only inferior in fire-power. For while the guerrilla group can tap the aid of the people, the army can only tap the aid of the few special interests and bureaucrats who run the country, often aided in their turn by a foreign power. In a situation where the people, or at least the local population, back the rebel force, the guerrillas should win.

Thus the guerrilla fighter is more than a guerrilla. He is a social reformer, who takes up arms for the people and fights to change the government. To be efficient, he must have detailed knowledge of his area of operation, so that he can withdraw rapidly and hide with ease. He must also never engage in an action unless certain to succeed, use all the weak points of his enemy, and stick to a strategy of 'strike and get out.' By its nature, guerrilla warfare is an early stage of classical warfare and cannot, by itself, win a war. But it is the training ground, which develops a nucleus of rebels into a small army, capable of fighting regular battles against the army of the oppressor. As each guerrilla is 'his own general,' it is his duty to protect his own life as carefully as a general does. Here Che makes an interesting distinction between the ordinary soldier and the guerrilla fighter. 'Each guerrilla must be ready to die, not to defend an ideal, but to transform it into a reality.'

As the regular army's aim is to destroy each and every guerrilla, the guerrilla's first aim is to discover the army's strategy and to thwart it. The defeat of that army is his long-term aim. His main supply of weapons will come from the army he fights, so that the enemy will help to destroy itself. It is better, indeed, to use the same weapons as the enemy, so that ammunition can be captured and used against the enemy. The whole guerrilla campaign should be planned in three phases:

1. Survival and adaptation to conditions of guerrilla life.

2. Erosion of enemy strength in the area marked out by the guerrilla group for its own territory.

3. Attacks on the enemy on his own ground, concentrating blows on communications and bases.

Che's rules for the campaign are emphatic. Strike the enemy constantly. Give him the impression that *he* is being harrassed and encircled. Teach the local population the aims of the guerrilla band, so that the people can see their advantage in aiding the insurrection. Use sabotage to demoralize the enemy and paralyse him by cutting off his communications. Avoid useless acts of terrorism. Do not try to hold too much territory. Create new guerrilla groups when sufficient recruits join. These new groups will hold more territory, until the offensive against the army on its own ground can start.

In all conditions, tactics must be adapted to circumstances. The guerrilla force must constantly improvise and transform all incidents to its own advantage. Classical war must be left to the enemy, the guerrillas must be unpredictable. Speed must characterize all assaults. 'The essential elements of the guerrilla group are surprise, deception and night operations.' Ambushes and the use of mines will bring in most captured weapons. The guerrilla group must be 'implacable' in attack, also in treating murderers and torturers. But it must be merciful to enemy soldiers; it must free prisoners and care for the enemy wounded. It must also show great consideration for the civilian population and local customs. In this way, it will prove its *moral* superiority over the enemy.

Che's *Guerrilla Warfare* continues by examining different strategies for fighting on favourable ground, unfavourable ground and urban areas. He discusses what types of arms should be used in each area, the number of men advisable and the tactics dictated by geography. Favourable ground is unsuitable for sabotage, capturing weapons and getting supplies. Unfavourable ground demands a campaign of great mobility. Action in urban areas can only be part of an overall strategy and must be directed wholly from *outside* the cities. Che concludes this section of his book by stressing the primacy of the countryside as a base for all guerrilla operations. Urban risings should only take place when the war in the rural areas needs support.

In the second part of his work, Che develops his theme of the nature of the guerrilla and of the guerrilla group. The guerrilla's role as an agrarian reformer and as 'a crusader for the people's freedom' is further defined. Each guerrilla must show impeccable moral conduct and strict self-control. 'He must be an ascetic . . . and must always aid the peasant technically, economically, morally and culturally.' This behaviour anticipates the guerrilla's role after the war is won, when the reform of the social structure will become a natural continuation of the guerrilla war itself.

In the same way, the guerrilla anticipates his future control of the means of justice and law by punishing traitors, by expropriating surplus land and livestock to redistribute to the poorer peasants, and by confiscating the property and businesses of the enemies of the revolution. He must also try to establish co-operatives, if possible, and to indoctrinate the local population ideologically. At this stage, there will be an interaction between the guerrillas and the peasants. The guerrilla, who is often an educated man of middle-class origins, will use his superior learning to enlighten the peasants, while the peasants will show him the *reality* of their social condition, a reality which the guerrilla has only known before in an abstract way. The peasants can also give a practical lesson to the guerrilla, teaching him what reforms are most needed.

Che goes on to describe the moral, physical and mental qualities needed by the guerrilla; they are an odd mixture of exalted virtues and expedient ones such as slyness, prudence, optimism, discretion, hardness. Every quality is called for: the guerrilla must be tireless, heroic, stoical, resilient, healthy ... and more. He must be ready to endure every privation, hunger, thirst, illness, wounds, fatigue and torture. After this catalogue of trials, Che concedes that, to endure so much, the guerrilla must be sustained by an ideal: 'This ideal must be simple, direct, not elaborate nor visionary. But it must be so firm and so clear that a man can, without the least hesitation, sacrifice his life for it.' The ideal may not be very lofty; for the peasant, owning land; for the workers, better wages. If anything, Che implies that, the more concrete the goal, the firmer the resolution of the guerrilla.

Che goes on to the practical aspects of guerrilla life, treating every side of the matter. His analysis reduces the needs of a guerrilla group to a basic minimum, except for three superfluities which were essential to Che himself—

tobacco, books to read and a notebook to record thoughts and events. Che's practical nature makes him describe even the shape of the most useful kind of knapsack. His Cuban experience is vital to his analysis of guerrilla equipment, as it is in his description of the three-stage guerrilla campaign that moves from the nomadic beginning to the semi-nomadic period of recruitment and finally to the permanent base-camps and frontal attacks of the last phase. Che adds little here to his previous writing on the Cuban Revolutionary War, except to emphasize the making of the guerrillas' own territory into a little state and a base of operations for sorties into enemy territory to capture heavy weapons, such as artillery and tanks. He also examines the concept of civilian action, and splits it into two categories. Within guerrilla territory, it is a question of government and indoctrination; but outside guerrilla ground, civilian action lies mainly in raising funds, making propaganda, gaining sympathizers and information, and carrying out sabotage.

Che then discusses the role of women in a guerrilla war. He first denounces the 'colonial mentality' of Latin Americans, who underestimate women to the point of discriminating against them. In fact, women make fine fighters and can also service the guerrilla group, acting as tailors and cooks and nurses. In civilian action, they are important as teachers and, above all, as couriers, taking messages between rebel and government territory. The presence of women should not lead to sexual rivalry among the guerrillas. A woman guerrilla should behave with the moral education of all guerrillas, although Che sees no reason why a revolutionary man and woman should not sleep together, if they are 'in love and have no other commitments.'

The role of the guerrilla doctor is particularly important to Che. Psychologically, especially in the early days of the group, the doctor is all-important as a source of strength to the wounded and to the ill. Medicines are less important than comfort. 'For a man in pain, a simple aspirin takes on importance when it is administered by the friendly hand of somebody who feels and identifies with the man's suffering.' Che then continues into a technical description of the creation of elementary hospitals, the use of stretcher-bearers, the performance of operations in the field and the other functions of healing in war.

Che then deals with propaganda, which he largely defines in the terms of reporting news. Rebel newspapers and radio must tell the truth at all costs. The object of the guerrilla media must be to tell the facts of battles and growing strength, because the government media will certainly be lying. The social programme of the guerrillas must also be explained. Getting information about the enemy is another necessity; peasants often make bad informers, and women good ones.

Che goes on to examine the training of recruits and the structure of the guerrilla force. Unlike the system in Latin American regular armies, promotion should only be given to men who deserve the rank and win it in combat. No guerrilla force can succeed without a great leader, who gives it sufficient time for training in absolute secrecy. For a guerrilla force must not only exist to beat the regular army and overthrow the government; it must also defend power after the Revolution is won. The regular army must be disbanded and a people's army created in its place, made up of peasants and workers and soldiers.

In the last chapter of *Guerrilla Warfare*, Che analyses the present and future situation in Cuba. He describes what the Revolutionary Government has done since it came into power, and demonstrates how these actions are the logical outcome of the war itself. Inevitably, these radical reforms have led to a break with the imperialist power which used to control Cuba, the United States, but Cuba no longer needs nor fears the United States. No countries which liberate themselves need fear the past colonial or neo-colonial powers which they may alienate. Che describes the sanctions and pressures exerted on Cuba by North American policy and denies that they can wreck the Cuban economy. Perhaps the United States may invade and inflict damage on the Cuban army, navy and air force. But the Revolution will survive such an attack, because it has kept its promises to the Cuban people who will defend the Revolution to the death.

This last chapter is not a mere patriotic harangue, although it was written in the tense period before the Bay of Pigs invasion of April, 1961. Che has a more important point to make : a revolution can withstand danger from the outside and from the inside only if it rapidly sets about keeping its promises to the people, so that they identify with it completely and feel that *their* survival is conditional on its survival. As soon as a successful guerrilla war has brought about a revolution, the whole population must be made revolutionary and must be given arms to defend what it has acquired. In this way, even if threatened from the outside by a superior force, the whole nation will become one vast guerrilla army defending every inch of ground with the same determination shown by the original guerrilla nucleus. In stating this, Che is remembering the Guatemalan fiasco, where the people had not been sufficiently armed to defend Arbenz's revolutionary régime.

Guerrilla Warfare has less appeal for Western intellectuals than Che's writings on socialist theory. It has little application to their situation and expresses few challenging ideas. It has, however, more significance for the Third World than any other of Che's writings, except for his later message to the Tricontinental Congress. When South American, African and Asian revolutionaries think of Che, when militant North American blacks think of Che, they think of this book. Apart from giving them a complete step-by-step course in guerrilla warfare as a method, it constantly repeats the same message. What has been done in Cuba can be done elsewhere, anywhere, whatever the odds.

Revolutionaries must not listen to the traditional Communist parties nor to other left-wing elements who harp about the right time and conditions, but never get on with the actual business of trying to seize power. Forget about parties and doctrines and theories, Che is saying, because only a few men are needed, a few guns, this manual and the determination to win. What a few Cubans did, all can do. Neither popular support nor a doctrine is really necessary. If the country is poor enough, the people will support the guerrillas as soon as the guerrillas begin to operate. The fighting of a war of liberation will teach the guerrillas whatever doctrine is the right one for them. Revolution feeds upon itself.

Elsewhere, Che conceded that the Cuban Revolution had three special factors working in its favour: the leadership of Fidel Castro, the unpreparedness of the United States and the class consciousness of the Cuban peasants who had suffered from the plantation system. Even so, Che maintained that the Cuban Revolution was no rare case. It could happen elsewhere. The basic factors were to be found in other underdeveloped or semi-developed countries. If one favourable factor was missing, another one would probably aid new guerrillas. The Cuban example was global and applicable.

Critics of *Guerrilla Warfare* have called the book wise after the event. It seems to rationalize improvised responses to situations beyond Fidel Castro's control. Che never denied this criticism, for analysis is the rationalization of past success and failure. What he did deny was that the Cuban experience was unique and insular. The Cuban War might have been the basis for nearly all Che's theories, but he thought that nearly all the world could study and apply the Cuban experience.

Herbert Matthews has said of Régis Debray's famous *Revolution in the Revolution?* that the book is almost a paraphrase of Che's writings, which in turn come from

Fidel Castro's experiences and ideas. There is no doubt that
Debray was Che's best pupil, and that Che and Fidel agreed
largely on the points made in *Guerrilla Warfare*—the basis
of Fidel's foreign policy in Latin America. Yet the military
strategy in the book resulted from the shared experience of
both men; Che spent the last months of the war as the
independent chief of a guerrilla column in charge of cutting
the island in two and effectively making his own decisions.
The important fact is that Che related the Cuban experience to a world-wide context. He was the theorist after the
war, if not the principal strategist during the war.

It is impossible to calculate whether Che or Fidel was the
greater military leader. They were symbiotic. *Guerrilla
Warfare* is a distillation of Che's original ideas and Fidel's
original ideas, based on conclusions that must have seemed
self-evident to all the men and women who fought in the
Cuban War. They all believed that revolutions could be
started and won in almost every Latin American country,
and that Fidel was speaking for all of them when he later
said that the Cordillera of the Andes had to be turned into
the Sierra Maestra of South America. Che sought to demonstrate that this was feasible by writing a manual and by
fighting later in Bolivia. That his manual was successful is
unquestionable. Now it even serves as a text-book for the
Green Berets and other North American counterinsurgency
special forces.

Yet Che is finally distinct less as a teacher of action than
as a philosopher of revolution. As Fidel said in his eulogy to
Che on October 18, 1967:

> ... When we think of Che, we do not think fundament-
> ally of his military virtues. No! Warfare is a means and
> not an end. Warfare is a tool of revolutionaries. The im-
> portant thing is the revolution, the revolutionary cause,
> revolutionary ideas, revolutionary objectives, revolu-
> tionary sentiments, revolutionary virtues.

Guerrilla Warfare is only incidentally a manual; it is chiefly a challenge to other theorists of revolution. Its three basic concepts, that popular forces can defeat armies, that the revolutionary focus can expand to create a total revolution and that the revolution is to be won from the countryside, are an open defiance of the theories of the Bolsheviks and other Communist parties. In the context of the Sino-Soviet split, these concepts have proved to be very dangerous.

Frequent comparisons have been made between Mao Tse-Tung's and Che's theories of guerrilla war. The primacy of guerrilla methods and of the countryside as the area of operations are common to both. Yet Che and other Cuban revolutionaries always insisted that they won their war against Batista without knowledge of the Chinese experience. This is probably a true statement, even if the Cubans were bound to stress the unique nature of their rising; there are enough parallels between the Cuban and the Chinese struggle to assume that their leaders would have drawn similar conclusions. Both insurrections began in the cities, where they failed to get support and lost to the regular army in actual combat. Both continued in rural areas, where they gained local support and began to defeat the regular army. This led to both making agrarian reform their chief revolutionary pledge and putting the peasants in the place of the urban proletariat as the new revolutionary class of China and Cuba.

The fact that the Cuban revolutionaries won *without* the support of the Cuban Communist Party, and the fact that they won long before they themselves turned to Communism as an ideology, accounts for the chief unorthodoxy of Che's writings in *Guerrilla Warfare*. Even the Chinese have never dared to put forward such a heresy. For Che's Cuban experience made him preach the autonomy of the guerrilla group *outside* the central control of the monolithic Communist parties, usually based in the cities. This theory was to be elaborated still further by Debray in *Revolution in the Revolution?* It is reminiscent of one of the issues that led to the break between the Anarchists and the Marxists in the 19th century. Should a revolutionary struggle be directed by a central party organization or by those who are actually doing the fighting on the spot?

This heresy of the Cubans also sprang from Che's glorification of the guerrilla himself. In an article written in 1959, called 'What is a Guerrilla Fighter?', Che gave an almost celestial vision of this perfect hero, as 'a sort of guiding angel who has fallen into the area, always to help the poor and to bother the rich as little as possible ...' Thus the guerrilla fighter is nearly divine, an unearthly gift dropped from the heavens, a Robin Hood or a saviour, a knight of chivalry who is magnanimous even to his enemies. If these visions are added to the technical, cultural, moral and ascetic qualities also defined by Che as necessary for the guerrilla, then the image of the guerrilla has replaced that of the saint. This idealized concept of the *guerrillero* is far from the concept of the starving, dirty, illiterate and dangerous *desperado*, lurking in the jungles to ambush and subvert, a sort of wild beast with a cause. It is very like the difference between the fact of the Spanish *conquistadors* and the images of the militant Christian saints, which they set up in the Catholic cathedrals of the Americas, in order to justify their past actions.

The idealization of the guerrillas had a political meaning. It helped Fidel Castro and his close comrades from the Sierra Maestra to take over all the key posts in the new government after the fall of Batista. They could justify themselves for forcing out all the politicians and the moderates who had not fought in the mountains. Thus Che's idealization of the guerrilla hero is a rationalization for the guerrillas' total seizure of power in Cuba. As Che once wrote: 'For a soldier of the liberation, the best training is guerrilla life itself. A leader who has not learned his difficult task in the daily exercise of arms is not an authentic leader.' This idea was noted by Debray, when he wrote of the men who fought in the Sierra Maestra : 'Strategically they risked everything, to win everything; at the end, they deserved to get everything.' The leaders of the Communist Party of Cuba had not risked everything, nor had the political exiles, nor had the democratic groups which opposed Batista. Therefore, they did not deserve to lead the new Cuba. They only deserved to serve under those who had actually won the victory in combat.

In his article of 1959, Che called the armed victory of the Cuban people 'a modifier of old dogmas.' The old dogmas were those of the men who called themselves revolutionaries, yet delayed the actual start of the fighting until an ideal moment which never came. They sought the red flag at the end of the rainbow. These false revolutionaries were explicitly the traditional Communist parties of Latin America. Thus Che began a controversy that has raged ever since, between the backers of the 'peaceful' or the 'violent' method of taking power. In a sense, Che's doctrine of the immediate guerrilla attack has broken up the traditional Communist parties of Latin America even more effectively than the military governments which have persecuted them. As Che always knew, an idea can be more dangerous than a regiment.

In Latin America, the followers of Guevara's theories have broken away from the orthodox Communist parties. The Cuban example has been more divisive in Latin American radical circles than even the split between Russia and China, although the Russians have tended to back the supporters of a 'peaceful' change of government through strikes and agitation and infiltration, while the Chinese have become the supporters of a 'violent' change through guerrilla insurrection. The controversy has weakened and split the radicals. It may have set back the clock of revolution by a few years. It certainly contributed to Che's own defeat and death in Bolivia. But it is a necessary quarrel for the future of the subcontinent.

Of the three major theorists of the immediate guerrilla assault—Castro, Guevara and Debray—Che seems to have been the most important. He was the first to raise the issue, the first to risk everything to prove his case correct, the first to die for his theories. The old guard of the Latin American Communists may survive the ideological attacks contained in *Guerrilla Warfare*, and they may live to see more attempts at Cuban-style revolutions defeated by government forces; but they probably will not survive their accusation by the personal example of Che himself. His return to the fight and his death have been their condemnation.

Guerrilla Warfare has been more immediately explosive than the *Communist Manifesto* was in its time. Following Che's writings and example, small handfuls of determined men and students have begun their own wars of liberation, sometimes choosing cities and universities in developed countries as battle-grounds rather than mountains and jungles. If they should win, they are provided by Che with a justification for seizing the whole apparatus of government and for ignoring charges of opportunism, made by democratic institutions and the existing political parties. The rebels are given a further justification for flouting the will of the particular Communist party of their own country, for their right and duty makes them substitute their own guerrilla organization for the stale hierarchy of the aging traditional party rulers. According to Che, the small rebel group should fight, should win and should rule, with the support of the people. Governments and old parties, which have lost the support of the people, should be defeated or denied. The guerrilla makes the leader, the revolution makes itself.

4 The Change in the Cuban Revolution

Fidel Castro set the task of the young revolutionaries who entered Havana with him on the overthrow of Batista in 1959. When he had been released from jail by Batista five years previously, he had declared: 'Our freedom will not be a fiesta nor a rest, but a struggle and a duty . . .' Most of Fidel's comrades were ill-equipped for the struggle and the duty of administering a country; but Che was one of the few exceptions. Even if he had no practical experience of economics, diplomacy, administration or politics, he was an educated and philosophical man, who had already shown managerial skills in the Sierra Maestra—unlike the courageous but nearly illiterate heroes, Juan Almeida and Camilo Cienfuegos. Yet Che's actual jobs within the Castro government were to be less important than the lessons which he learned from them and applied within them. Just as he was the theoretician of the war, so he was the theoretician of the administration.

There are conflicting points of view about Che's importance to Fidel Castro's régime. Some critics of the régime see him as the *éminence grise*, the only man who could construct an ideology and a programme for the Revolution in a consistent and orderly way. Fidel's own sister, Juana, who emigrated from the island after the Revolution, has always asserted with other witnesses that it was Che who actually converted the guerrillas to Communism as a doctrine. Other historians of Cuba have attributed less importance to Che, see nothing essential in his influence on the course of the Cuban experiment and consider most of his theories as retrospective assertions of other people's ideas and actions. To them, Che is the Boswell of the Cuban Revolution.

The truth seems to lie between the two extremes. For Che certainly contributed to the Revolution almost as much as Fidel Castro did. Without Che's observant analysis and occasional eloquence, shown in such pieces as his important *Man and Socialism in Cuba*, the Cuban Revolution would have lacked both definition and utopianism. Fidel was a lawyer and a leader. For him, the laws and the pleas and the set speeches of attack and defence, with the people as the jury. But Che was a doctor. For him, the diagnosis and the cure, the meaning of life and death.

The position of Fidel and Che within Cuba also dictated different attitudes. As the *jefe maximo*, Fidel had to keep the Revolution going and the economy of the island above water. He had to make the political deals necessary for internal security and external loans. He had to balance the conflicting forces among his followers and to listen to the wishes and complaints of the Cuban people. He had to bluff and trade for Russian support, and never to provoke the United States to the point of intervention. His pre-occupations were with the daily business of running a country.

While Fidel dealt with the problems as they arose, both in the Sierra Maestra and later in Havana, his subordinate Che could concentrate on finding a theory for what he thought had to be done. The testimony of reporters makes it plain that Fidel Castro did not foresee the shape of his future government while he was still fighting in the mountains. As Herbert Matthews wrote : 'Fidel naïvely (to use his own word to me) believed that the rebels could make a radical social revolution democratically. Since his basic aim was revolution, and democracy was simply the method that he thought he could use, when the crunch came he changed his method, not his goal.' As Che was always the extremist on the left of the guerrilla leaders, Fidel's break with the democratic process and supposed 'betrayal' of the

aims of the Revolution was partially the result of Fidel
taking Che's advice.

In the first year of the Revolution, Fidel and his movement helped to set up a government of moderate, liberal,
middle-aged men with a record of integrity and opposition
to Batista. This liberal group immediately began to clash
with the more radical group of guerrilla leaders, who felt
that they had many promises to keep to the Cuban
peasants, and that radical reform demanded draconian
measures. Soon Fidel had squeezed out all the moderates
and had replaced them with comrades from the Sierra
Maestra. As Celia Sánchez testified, the rebels had thought
they would have to govern through moderates; but they
soon found out that they were the masters of the island. At
that moment, Che's concept of guerrilla government made
sense. The opportunity chose its theory. If radical changes
were to be made, only the guerrilla leaders could make
them.

An analysis of the six years Che spent in Cuba after 1959
is really a history of the Cuban Revolution. When Jean-Paul
Sartre called Che 'the most complete man of his age,' he
was stating that Che so lived his own words and so spoke
his own actions that his own history and his own society
told much the same story. The complexity of the Cuban
Revolution, its dedication and its originality, its experiments and its failures, serve as a dark mirror to Che
Guevara. While Che was helping to fashion the Revolution,
the Revolution was helping to fashion him. But in six areas,
Che's writing and doing was essential for the Cuban experiment—in agriculture, industry, monetary policy, moral incentives, revolutionary conscience and international affairs.

Cuba was mainly an agrarian society. Thus the Cuban
Revolution had to be mainly an agrarian revolution. The
economy of the island as well as the emotion of the fighters
from the Sierra Maestra dictated the policy that the
countryside came first. Three-quarters of Cuba's foreign

earnings came from the sale of sugar alone. The sugar
harvest was the condition of Cuban prosperity. Yet the
landless labourers who brought in the sugar were treated
less well than cattle, while the urban workers were relatively privileged. The revolution needed the support and the
work of the peasants. Memories of the mountain war and
Che's glorification of the peasants as *the* revolutionary class
were merely the sentiments behind a political need.
Agrarian reform had already been started in the areas held
by the rebels. Now that they held the whole island, that
reform should encompass the whole island.

Che is explicit on the way in which the needs and the
policies of the guerrillas and the peasants interacted:

> The men who arrived in Havana after two years of
> hard struggle in the mountains and plains of Oriente, in
> the lowlands of Camuguey, and in the mountains, plains
> and cities of Las Villas, were not the same men ideo-
> logically, who landed on the beaches of Las Coloradoas,
> or who took part in the first phase of the struggle. Their
> distrust for the peasant had been converted into affection
> and respect for his virtues; their total ignorance of life in
> the country had been converted into a knowledge of the
> needs of our landless labourers; their flirtation with statis-
> tics and with theory had been solidified by the cement
> which is practice. With the banner of agrarian reform,
> the execution of which began in the Sierra Maestra, these
> men confronted imperialism. They knew that agrarian
> reform would give land to all the dispossessed, and that it
> would dispossess its unjust possessors ... We learned
> from the peasants that there is no limit to the efforts, to
> the sacrifice that we can all make when we are fighting
> for the destiny of the people.

In this key passage, Che was making three vital points, that
the peasants themselves had shaped the guerrillas, that land
reform had already begun during the war and that the

logical end of land reform was the attack on imperialism. Agrarian reform was a guerrilla faith, a necessity at home and a policy abroad.

Thus the most important law put out by the new revolutionary government was the First Agrarian Reform of May, 1959. The plantations, large farms and major properties were all nationalized. Emphasis was placed on moving from a one-crop economy to diversity in agriculture. Full employment all the year round was the aim. Cooperative and state farms were set up as examples and small farmers, who still kept their land, were given credit and were taught improved methods for cultivating the soil. Che described the effect on Cuban society of this first reform :

> *Radical, agrarian reform, the only type which can give* . *land to the peasant, collides directly with the interests of the imperialists, large landowners and sugar and ranching magnates. The bourgeoisie is afraid of colliding with those interests. The proletariat is not. Thus the process of the revolution unites the workers and the peasants. The workers support the demands made against large landholders. The poor peasant, given control of the land, loyally supports revolutionary power and defends it against imperialist and counter-revolutionary enemies.*

This statement showed the development in Che's thought and in the Cuban Revolution. Che had decided that there were two classes which supported the Revolution; the peasants, who had helped so loyally in the early battles, and the urban workers, who now helped to defend the peasants in the later stages of the Revolution against their mutual enemies—the landowners, the foreign interests and the *bourgeoisie*, a class which radical reform was beginning to turn against the Revolution. Before this stage, the Revolution had been termed classless. The peasants had been called the 'vanguard class'; but this definition had not excluded the 'good bourgeois,' who had contributed, after all, most of

49

the guerrilla leaders and their urban sympathizers. Nor had it excluded the industrial workers, although they had contributed little to the defeat of Batista, and although their support had been lukewarm during the war.

The Cuban Communists, indeed, had been disconcerted by the classless nature of the successful Revolution. As the Communist Juan Marinello conceded in January, 1959, 'The triumphant Revolution has not been the work of one party, one class or of one group. The people have gained the victory.' Fidel had concurred with this judgement. According to him, the Revolution had been won 'with the help of men of all ideas, of all religions, of all social classes.' It 'belonged to all' and 'had admirably united the people.' It was Che who had preferred to emphasize the role of the peasants as a class; and now agrarian reform ushered in the concept of a class struggle. It divided Cuban society into two camps; on one side, the landowners supported by much of the middle class which feared its own later expropriation; on the other side, the peasants, now supported by the urban workers.

These events coincided with the turning of the Cuban leaders towards Marxism–Leninism, with their *rapprochement* with the Cuban Communist Party, with their worsening relationship with the United States after the nationalization of North American-owned plantations, and with their new friendship with the Soviet Union, delighted to extend its influence so close to the shores of Florida. Moreover, the urban workers were beginning to realize that they might also benefit from this rural revolution, while the middle class was increasingly alienated by Fidel's break with the old democratic leaders and with the United States, for long the chief influence on the Cuban *bourgeoisie*.

In this shift of government policy, Che was the instigator and theorist. The shift met with the evolution in his thinking that had begun in Guatemala, had developed in Mexico City, and had formed in the Sierra Maestra. The revolutionary war against Batista and his tyranny had, for a time, made him concentrate his hate against a personal enemy and his henchmen. Despotism had a particular face. But soon after the victory, Che turned his back on this feud. Foreign imperialism again became the real enemy, as it had been in Guatemala. The only lasting solution to the problems of underdeveloped countries, their only defence against the economic power of imperialism, seemed to lie more in the creation of industries than in the development of agriculture, however just the rational distribution of land might be to the poor peasant.

Soon the emphasis in Che's speeches began to alter. There was less said about the peasant, more about the workers; less said about land reform, more about new industries. By October, 1959, Che was head of the industrial department of reorganization; then, after serving as Director of the National Bank, he was made Minister of Industry in February, 1961. His early function was to oversee the conversion of agricultural products and wastes into industrial products; his later function was to spawn new processes to make Cuba self-sufficient. Underdevelopment became his bogey:

What is underdevelopment?
A dwarf with an enormous head and a swollen chest is 'underdeveloped,' to the degree that his weak legs or his short arms do not coordinate with the rest of his body . . . We are countries with economies distorted by the action of imperialism, which has abnormally developed the industrial or agricultural resources necessary to complement its complex economy. 'Underdevelopment' or distorted development carries with it a dangerous specialization in raw materials, containing a threat of hunger for all our people. We, 'the underdeveloped,' are those of the single crop, the single produce and the single market. A single product, with an uncertain sale which depends

> *upon a single market that imposes and sets conditions—*
> *This is the great formula of imperial economic domina-*
> *tion which is combined with the old and always useful*
> *Roman formula: Divide and rule.*

The fact that the Cuban economy had been tied to the sugar import quota set by the Congress of the United States merely proved Che's point about underdeveloped countries.

Che did not feel that he was deserting the peasants in his new emphasis on the workers of the cities. The peasantry was to be rewarded with land reform, social benefits, full employment, education, mechanization and crop diversification. Yet now, only one class could free Cuba from its underdevelopment, the urban workers. It was their turn to become the 'vanguard class' of the Revolution. The *bourgeoisie* was doomed by 1961. Che would concede no more to previous middle-class support against Batista than that the *bourgeoisie* had been briefly disoriented during the war, 'even looking sympathetically upon the actions of the rebels due to the pressure of imperialism upon their interests.'

A new war had to be declared on the middle class. And here Che revealed openly how much the example of the *conquistadors* had mattered to the dozen guerrillas who had survived to conquer a whole island, just as Pizarro had survived with thirteen men on the isle of Gallo before conquering the whole of Peru. Pizarro had drawn a line on the sand, over which only a handful had stepped, while the rest of his force had turned back in defeatism and despair. But Pizarro's small group had endured to win Peru, just as Fidel's group had endured to win Cuba. And now the example of the great *conquistador* of the Incas was conjured up by Che to explain his attack on the new enemies of the Revolution. 'Cuba has drawn the line in the sand again, and again we see Pizarro's dilemma: on the one hand, there are those who love the people, and on the other, those who hate the people. Between them, each time a bit more explicitly, the line divides the two great social forces, the *bourgeoisie* and the working class, which are defining with increasing clarity their respective positions as the process of the Cuban Revolution advances.'

As always, Che dated his pre-occupation with new industries back to the experiences in the Sierra Maestra. He declared, 'Fidel remembered how in the Sierra we had once set up a small shoe factory, and from that time we became industrialists.' The setting up of industries now became part of the guerrilla struggle and of the global fight for the liberation of the Third World. 'Cuba's great impact has been as a political force—as the embodiment of all underdeveloped countries struggling for their freedom. The two elements of revolution are interrelated—the goal of those countries fighting for their freedom is to become industrialized in order to gain that freedom.' For the Third World, the guerrilla struggle was only the prelude to the industrial struggle against economic imperialism.

Naturally, the industrial struggle demanded of the Cuban worker many of the qualities necessary for the guerrilla. The urban workers had to acquire the same dedication and spirit of self-sacrifice that the rural fighter had possessed. The peasants had fought and won the first stage of the Revolution. Thus they were receiving their reward, the land and its right use. Now the workers had to fight the second stage of the Revolution, the creation of a home industrial base. While this was being done, the workers must sacrifice many of the economic benefits which they already had, particularly the wages which gave them a standard of living many times greater than the rural labourer. The workers must now carry forward the self-sacrifice of the Revolution. They must not see in the new state merely another boss and a stingier boss. As their standard of living was bound to drop before it improved again, the workers had to identify their hopes for a prosperous future for themselves and their children on the success of the Revolution. And they had better do so gladly, in order to make their sacrifices worthwhile.

Che's critics find his switch of emphasis cynical. When he needed the support of the peasants, he called for their self-sacrifice and backed agrarian reform. But when he needed the urban workers more than the peasants, he called for their self-sacrifice in the name of industrial growth. During the first stage, hatred of the landowners forged a bond between the guerrillas and the peasants; during the second stage, the *bourgeoisie* was attacked in order to appease the workers. In both cases, the theory and the ideology seemed to be justifications of *realpolitik*; for instance, the local Communist Party was courted when its strength in the labour unions was needed to keep the urban workers from striking. Che appeared merely to be adding a gloss of concept to a smart strategy worthy of any politician.

Yet experience and analysis, practice and plan are inextricably connected. Che's political progress and the political progress of Cuba kept pace during the first years of revolutionary government. The interaction between Che's ideology and public policy was almost a marriage of aims. A chart can even be made of the change in Che's personal views and in the aims of the Revolution. Events may have dictated much of that change; but Che's ideology played its part. And the progress and process of every great revolution demand the appearance of a consistent policy and ideology, successfully pursued.

The Change in the Cuban Revolution

	Early Position	Later Position
Scene of the struggle	The Sierra Maestra and the rural areas	The whole of Cuba with the emphasis on the cities
Leaders	The guerrillas as a military force outside politics	The guerrillas as the political masters
Allies	Peasants and middle-class urban reformers	Communists, urban workers and peasants
Enemies	Batista, the regular army, large Cuban and North American interests	The United States and the growing colony of Cuban exiles there
Vanguard Class	The peasants	The urban proletariat
Priorities	Redistribution of the land, diversification of agriculture	Nationalization of industry, development of technology, full use of resources
Trade and Diplomacy	Latin America, the United States and Western Europe	Soviet Russia and Eastern Europe
Ideology	'Humanistic democracy on the basis of liberty with bread for all peoples.' *Fidel Castro, 1959*	'I am a Marxist–Leninist and shall be until the day I die.' *Fidel Castro, 1961*

5 An End to Money

Both in theory and practice, Che Guevara despised money. His personal life had always been a reproach to greed. He seemed to get as much satisfaction from doing without money as most individuals get from spending it. His personal asceticism led him to a primitive communism, in which money was an unnecessary evil. He loathed cash as a medieval monk loathed usury. From his youth, his scorn was chiefly reserved for those who spent their whole time in piling up a fortune. And in his farewell letter to Fidel, there is a quiet pride in his assertion: 'I have left no material possessions to my wife and children, and I do not regret it. I am happy that it is this way.' To most men, this admission would be humiliating; to Che, it was a source of pride. How many other Latin American politicians could say the same on leaving office? And how many of them had worked for a government so just that they need not worry about the future of a wife left with four small children to rear?

Che was not only opposed to greed in individuals, but also in enterprises and nations. He hated the principle of foreign loans; he thought they should be gifts. Such sentiments not only made Che the sworn enemy of capitalism and free enterprise, but also made him oppose many practices of the Soviet bloc, particularly Russia's loans at interest to Cuba. He was outraged by the fact that, in most societies, workers have to sell their labour and skills to the highest bidder. He could never accept that human beings or nations should be motivated by greed, so he opposed the method of material incentives to increase productivity, also the harsh workings of the law of supply and demand. He dreamed of the single wage-scale, in which everybody would earn the same wage or would earn according to his needs, until money could be abolished altogether. Public demand for a certain product or skill should not pay more for it than for another, less popular but socially more desirable.

Ironically enough, this arch-enemy of money was chosen to run the National Bank of Cuba, before he became Minister of Industry. Yet there was a perverse logic in the choice of Che. To fight prostitution, a reformer goes to the brothel, not to the home of a virtuous woman. To fight the old monetary system, a man becomes director of the national bank. Che's special concern, however, with industrialization in Cuba must have also had something to do with his decision. He had to get the loans and credits and subsidies to finance his projects for new factories and processes. Like the Good Woman of Setzuan, Che had to put on the mask of the wicked financier in order to keep the wheels of industry turning. With Macheath he could have pondered: What is robbing a bank compared with running a bank?

Before he took on his new job, Che had no more than an intelligent man's knowledge of economics. So he quickly educated himself in banking theory. He wrote many articles on finance, quoting Marxist and Hegelian sources to refute orthodox Communist and capitalist economists who defended or worked with the world's monetary system. Che's morals fundamentally dictated his economic theories; his learning was window-dressing. Although he taught himself the methods of banking, he wanted to use finance merely as a weapon to impose his ideology. To prove the ideology, the methods had to work. But the reasons for choosing one method rather than another were not economic; they were moral. Che's vision of the new Socialist Man was never far from his thoughts on revolution, warfare or economics. He was striving to create that new being and to end man's exploitation by man. Everything, including economics, had to serve in the birth of those ideals. Here lay Che's originality and influence.

Che believed that a revolutionary socialist government inherited a great many capitalist ways of thought alien to the purpose of the Revolution. These ways had to be blotted out at once, or they would corrupt the new comradeship and radicalism. It was not enough to turn the old system into a welfare state, to nationalize industries and to distribute wealth more justly. Marxism and central planning were more than a means to run a state more efficiently and fairly. Unless the new system could alter the relationship of men to each other and to their society, then all the struggle and suffering of the rebellion against the previous régime was not worth the dead and the maimed and the loss. Moreover, there would be another rebellion, if the new system was merely an improved model of the bad old ways.

For socialism to mean more than a higher standard of living for an exploited majority, the quality of life had to be bettered. A meaning for living had to be provided along with material advance. Above all, that meaning had to apply to man's labour. Socialism had to supply 'a future in which work will be man's greatest dignity, in which work will be a social duty as well as a true human pleasure and the ultimate act of creation.' While a man's labour was a mere commodity to be bought and sold, he could not see his work in these terms. It was 'a sad duty, an unfortunate necessity.' That was the true curse of capitalism; it alienated man from what should be the source of his greatest satisfaction, pride in his labour. By changing his pride in work well done to a quest for the cash rewards for output, capitalism had corrupted the dignity of the worker and had turned him into a greedy parody of himself, where he worked for what he could buy in his leisure time, not for the work itself. Change the worker's attitude towards his work and towards his rewards, and then the economy and the society and the man would change towards true social-ism.

Che felt that this problem had to be dealt with at once during the first fervour of revolutionary pride. He clashed here with the old-line Communists. They wanted to set up a socialist economy first of all; when it was successful, then a true socialist mentality would develop in the workers. Che disagreed. After fifty years of socialism in Soviet Russia, too many capitalist incentives and ways of thought still remained among workers and managers. Indoctrination should precede rewards for increased production. 'We affirm that, in a relatively short time, the development of conscience does more for the development of production than material incentive.' The development of conscience meant getting workers to work at full pressure by appealing not to their greed nor to their ambition nor to their fear, but to their idealism and to their belief in their leaders and to their longing for a better future for their whole community as well as for themselves. With the state looking after their every need, the workers could labour for the good of all, until money became as obsolete as slavery.

Che's Theory of Value, which Fidel supported, was the basis of the whole economic argument. Value was not defined according to supply and demand. Value was defined according to the moral and social worth of a product or service, not its worth on the market. Thus the value of work was more important in human terms than in terms of economic efficiency. The state bank should calculate the budget for enterprises according to their social value, not give loans to state monopolies run by managers obsessed by mere productivity, as in Russia. Che thought of value in its old moral sense, not its narrow economic definition. Economic man was a monster created by the capitalist system; man was the social and political being defined by the ancient Greek philosophers. The economic system should serve man's values by serving the values of his society.

Money was worth no part of a man's life.

This utopian Theory of Value governed Che's decision as manager of the National Bank. He thought it unfair to encourage competition between a state enterprise that manufactured beer and one that manufactured text-books, just because the beer sold far better than the text-books. To expand the beer industry because it was profitable was socially undesirable, if it meant less money to produce text-books. It was the duty of the National Bank to judge the relative value of the two products to Cuban society, and then to allot a budget to each enterprise, determined by the social value of the product rather than by the profit made by the Cuban state. Loans to enterprises were to be free of interest, to prevent any pressure being put on the enterprise which might corrupt its social purpose in the quest for profits. In the same way, workers must not be given a share of the enterprise's profits; otherwise, a class of privileged workers would be created who would earn more than other workers that benefited the whole community by labour in unprofitable enterprises. The reward of labour lay in the good of all. The National Bank must discourage undue competition and incentives, the twin brothers of greed. Its decision must teach the only true value, comradeship in the service of the Revolution.

These beliefs led Che to make difficult choices on the question of centralized planning. Obviously, local planning led to a greater feeling of participation, but it also led to competition among local areas. Central planning allowed planning for the good of the whole island; it also aided the introduction of better technology and processes. In one of his speeches defending the idea of centralized control, Che called capitalist competition 'a struggle among beasts' and localized socialist competition aiming at maximum profits 'a struggle among caged beasts.' Che would never be pragmatic over economic theory: he would rather be fanatic. He was after the fulfilment of men's spiritual wants; their

bodily needs were incidental. Even over such a socialist matter as volunteer work, Che wanted more than the
work itself. 'Volunteer work is not only a factor to aug-
ment production; it is the fountainhead of socialist education for the masses.'

Thus Che and his school of economists wanted central
planning with all profits returning to the state for distribution over the entire economy and society. Agriculture
should be run in the same way as industry; huge state farms
should employ all labourers permanently on a salary, and
profits should be ploughed back into the collectivity. The
dominant goal should be industrialization as the only
method of emancipating Cuba from a world market in
which the developed powers bought raw materials at low
cost and sold finished goods at high cost. Industrialization
was also the only cure for the underemployment that
plagued all underdeveloped countries. Agrarian reform was
essential as well, in order to move an underdeveloped
country from a one-crop economy to self-sufficiency, even
if this meant cutting down the basic crop which provided
foreign capital. Economic independence was the basis of
political independence.

The motive behind this programme was to be supplied by
revolutionary consciousness. 'The construction of socialism
is not work alone. The construction of socialism is not consciousness alone. It is work and consciousness, development
of material goods through work and development of consciousness.'　But the development of a revolutionary consciousness must be more important than the development of
production. For instance, although competition was bad in
capitalist or socialist states when it encouraged rivalry and
material differences, it was good when it encouraged true
comrades to work harder. Competition was a double-edged
sword. 'Competition cannot be like a ball-game where the
loser throws oranges at the referee. Competition should be
fraternal. Why? So that every one increases production. It

is a weapon to increase production. Not only that, but it is also an instrument to deepen the consciousness of the masses, and the two must always go together.' The same distinction applied to volunteer work, which was a form of education in which work ceased to be an obsession as in the capitalist world and became a pleasant social duty. The making of a new man was the prime aim of all social tasks.

The astounding fact about modern Cuba is that this ideal of Che's was put into practice. Whatever the enemies of the Cuban Revolution have said, volunteer work is still genuinely done by volunteers, even if their reasons for doing the work may not be Che's reasons. They may volunteer because everyone else does, or because they fear rebuke from their comrades, or because there is not much else to do with leisure time in Cuba. But still, revolutionary enthusiasm and consciousness do play their part. When the inhabitants of Havana voluntarily leave for their spell of cane-cutting during the sugar harvest, they feel that they are doing their special bit for the Revolution. They may work badly, lazily, inefficiently; but they work for their society. They prove Che right. It is possible to give ordinary people enough revolutionary consciousness to give them a meaning in their work. It is a step towards Che's ideal, when the worker shall work 'no longer just to make a living, but to build something which he sees and feels as his own.'

Yet Che was not completely dogmatic nor rigid in his thinking, even with all his emphasis on central planning. He did not want to build a powerful state, but a happy socialist people. In fact, he denounced those who thought in orthodox and set terms. 'The task of creating a socialist society in Cuba must be met by fleeing mechanical thinking like the plague; mechanical thinking only leads to stereotyped methods.' Marxism was a dialectic, a process of change. Sectarianism within Marxism was a disease, a refusal to experiment. To Che, the revolutionary had to remain a human being. 'Being human' meant to Che the opposite to being weak or behaving no better than most other humans. It meant acting for the best rather than for the least effort. Above all, it meant that a man should develop his sensibility, so that 'he feels anguish when a man is assassinated in any corner of the world, and he feels elation when in some corner of the world a new banner of liberty is raised.' Che found the words 'human' and 'revolutionary' the same. That was the conscience of the revolutionary.

There is no question that Che's economic thinking contained an element of contradiction. A streak of utopian anarchism and primitive Communism lay at the back of all his emphasis on central control. At one workers' rally, Che began his speech by quoting a poet who was lamenting that nobody had been able 'to dig the rhythm of the sun' nor to 'cut an ear of corn with love and grace.' Che then explained that the Cubans had left this sort of attitude behind them and had created a new one through their desire 'to return to nature, to change daily chores into meaningful play.' If the poet came back to Cuba, he would see 'how man, after passing through all the stages of capitalist alienation, and after being thought a beast of burden in harness to the yoke of the exploiter, has found his way back again to play. In Cuba today, work takes on a new meaning. It is done with a new happiness.' Che went on to stress there was, indeed, 'love and grace' in the very action of cutting sugar cane, and that the slavery of man did not lie in his need to work, but in his failure to own the means of production. But when man repossessed the means of production, he also regained his old sense of happiness in work. He felt himself important within the social mechanism.

He became happy to feel himself a cog in the wheel, a cog which has its own characteristics and is necessary, although not indispensable, to the production process, a conscious cog, a cog which has its own motor, and which

> consciously tries to push itself harder and harder to carry
> to a happy conclusion one of the premises of the con-
> struction of socialism—creating a sufficient quantity of
> consumer goods for the entire population.

Ironically enough, Che revealed himself in this speech to
be near the position of the original Puritan ethic which was
the motor for the North American economy. The Puritans
had always stressed that work was a social duty and should
be joyfully performed. As Herbert's hymn pointed out, the
man

> *Who sweeps a room as for Thy laws*
> *Makes that and the action fine.*

The laws of Che's society were not those of a 17th century
society; but the methods of persuading men to work hard
and happily at menial jobs were not different.

In his famous essay *Man and Socialism in Cuba*, Che
summed up his economic philosophy. He began by denying
that the Cuban state was setting out to extinguish the individual. It was setting out to create a new individual,
glimpsed in the days of heroic fighting in the Sierra Maestra
and in the days when the whole population had sacrificed
itself to serve the nation during the Missile Crisis and during
Hurricane Flora. The problem was to perpetuate the sense
of service that only came to the surface during days of
crisis or disaster. That sense depended on perfect communications between the people and its leaders. 'The initiative generally comes from Fidel or the high command of
the Revolution; it is explained to the people, who make it
their own. At times local experiences are taken up by the
party and the government and are thus generalized.' These
communications were not yet good enough, which explained certain failures in understanding; but they would
improve.

Of course, such a system of government appeared to

mean the subordination of the individual. But to Che, Western individualism meant no more than the rule of capitalism. To him, Rockefeller was the supreme individualist of the West. 'It is a race of wolves. He who arrives does so only at the expense of the failure of others.' In socialism, the individual was not a greedy being, but an unfinished product; Socialist society had to eradicate flaws of bad conditioning from the individual and the individual had to re-educate himself. He had to forget the twin ideas of capitalism—that the individual is isolated, and that relationships are governed by the law of supply and demand. Many underdeveloped countries which had freed themselves from imperialist control remained the pawns of the imperialists by failing to free themselves from capitalist assumptions. To build revolutionary consciousness, a new man had to be created simultaneously with a new material base for the nation.

Thus the new revolutionary society had to be a huge school. After all, capitalism might resort to force; but it also educated its people in the meaning of its system. The Cuban government had to indoctrinate its people even more intensively, because they had to unlearn the errors of capitalism. Only then could a new sort of man begin to emerge. His image was unfinished and would never be finished, because he was advancing parallel to the development of new economic forms. He no longer advanced *alone* towards vague personal longings. With the masses, he followed his party leaders towards the goals of the new society. He supported revolutionary institutions and sacrifices, but even they were only transitory stages towards the new world. The ultimate goal of the Revolution was to set men free from their alienation from their society, which they miscalled their individualism. 'In spite of the apparent standardization of man in socialism, he is more complete.'

Thus Che ignored the question of how the individual can oppose his society by stating that it was not a real question.

He agreed with Plato in saying that the realization of each man lay within his communistic society. Thus each man's voice must be heard within the social apparatus, not against it. All divisive tendencies that turned comrades into rivals must go—work for money, undue competition. Work must be a social duty, leaving time for the enriching of society by other pursuits. 'The machine is only the front line where duty is performed.' Freed by not having to work in order to feed and clothe and house his family, a man could see himself fulfilled in his work for the whole community. Che admitted that work in the socialist state still had to be partly coercive; but that coercion should be what Fidel called 'moral compulsion,' and that coercion would wither away when social conscience developed properly and generally.

Che thought that art really showed the difference between the capitalist and the socialist society. In capitalism, the artist attacked the state. 'Senseless anguish and vulgar pastimes are comfortable safety-valves for human uneasiness.' Yet the true revolution contained all artistic experimentation within itself. Admittedly, there were 'no artists of great authority who also have great revolutionary authority.' But the revolution was still young, experiment would find them and the new socialist man. Che scorned the social realism of the 19th century that was enshrined as the official art of Soviet Russia and China. That was reactionary, just as Western decadent art of the twentieth century was a reaction in itself from that dead realism. Bold and persistent experiments would find a new art fit for the new man of the twentieth century.

That new man would find his inspiration in the guerrilla leaders of the Cuban Revolution, particularly in their self-sacrifice. They were guided by authentic feelings of love, yet they had given up even their family life for the cause. 'There is no life outside the Revolution.' The people must follow their leaders' example towards true proletarian internationalism, a longing to help their exploited comrades all over the world. The leaders must educate the people towards this end. 'We are at the head of the people that is at the head of America.'

Che ended his greatest statement with a series of maxims to rally the Cuban people like bugle calls to the cause and the faith:

We Socialists are more free because we are more ful-filled: we are more fulfilled because we are more free . . .

Our sacrifice is a conscious one: it is in payment for the freedom we are building . . .

We will make the twenty-first century man: we our-selves.

So much for Che's early hopes and intentions. They were mostly disappointed. Even in Cuba, utopia was not just around the corner. In an article written in October, 1964, Che analysed the errors made by the Cuban government in agriculture and in industry. An expert at self-criticism, Che's judgement of his country's and his own mistakes was as harsh and as lucid as any enemy could have made. He had attacked the one-crop system as the bane of underdeveloped countries, and he had supported diversification in agriculture as the means to full rural employment and national self-sufficiency. Theoretically correct, the actual practice of the policy had been a failure. Too much diversification was attempted at once; there was a general decline in agricultural production. Thus Cuba had to return to its original role as a major producer of sugar, the basic economic fact of its existence. Che now conceded that the fetish that connected sugar with Cuba's dependence on imperialism and with misery in rural areas had been only a fetish. In fact, the truth was that the Cubans should produce sugar and get more money for it. Sugar was not the devil, the balance of trade was.

Similar errors had taken place in Cuba's immediate and

enthusiastic industrialization. Che admitted to a failure in understanding the precise technology and economics necessary in setting up new industries. Again, unemployment and a wish for national self-sufficiency had made the Cubans acquire too many factories too fast. The result was that the Cubans produced shoddy consumer goods at a high price by international standards. Even the problem of paying for imported consumer goods was not much helped, because the cost of importing raw materials was almost as high. Sadly and expensively, the new Cuban government had to learn the gap between ideology and practice. Che admitted his mistakes and the root cause of them. 'A group of young men who, without any previous experience, has to take command of an accelerated process of development in the face of the military and economic power of the so-called Western World is naturally going to make mistakes.'

An obsession with the need to industrialize and a determination to manufacture consumer goods at home rather than to import them were understandable errors for Cuba to make. After all, in Batista's time, the United States had bought nearly all of Cuba's sugar and had supplied nearly all of Cuba's goods. Now the United States had become Cuba's enemy and its past policy was anathema to Che. The North American economic blockade of the island, which effectively reduced the flow of Western goods to a trickle, had made Cuba dependent on goods that had to be supplied by the Eastern bloc several thousand miles away—hardly a good argument for refusing to try to make goods at home. The logic of past and present trading difficulties had forced Cuba to experiment with home production just as much as the ideology of the Cuban Revolution itself.

Che also confessed to theoretical errors in economic planning. These errors were of two contradictory kinds. One series of errors came from imitating the grandiose Russian Five Year Plans with their rigid stages of decision and unattainable production norms. The other series of errors sprang from snap decisions, made on the spot to push everything forward faster than it could go. These errors were aggravated by other factors: the shortage of spare parts for machinery that originally came from the United States, the irregular supplies of new machinery sent by the friendly nations in the Eastern bloc, the mass exodus of bourgeois managers and technicians, the lack of statistical and expert knowledge, and the priority given to expropriation and redistribution of wealth during the first few years of revolution. Che stressed other factors:

We had to keep our factories, our agriculture and our transportation going—without credits, without insecticides, without raw materials, without spare parts, without technicians, without organization. During this time outlaws operated in our territory, supported by the United States, and committed acts of sabotage and aggression. The constant threat of invasion forced us to mobilize the Cuban people two or three times a year, thus paralyzing the country ...

We did not owe all our planning mistakes to our decisions. We owed them also to the action of imperialism, which forced upon us a process of acceleration far beyond the best that the party was capable of doing. Despite our errors, we recorded considerable successes ...

If Che's economic theories were largely responsible for what went wrong in the Cuban economy, they were also largely responsible for what went right. The test of success does not lie only in practical results, as Che would have been the first to insist. The final proof of a government's performance lies in whether it keeps the support of the masses or not. By this proof Lyndon Johnson's Great Society did worse than the programme of the Cuban Revolution over its first six years. The Cuban people remained behind their government and its programme. The North American people did not.

Perhaps Fidel Castro has been one of the greatest mobilizers of hope that the world has ever seen; but Che has provided him with many of the thoughts for mobilizing that hope. Che was the great partisan of moral incentives and of the need not to sacrifice revolutionary consciousness to material incentives or economic efficiency. No skilled urban worker in Cuba today would still be supporting the government, if he had not learned to work for the building of socialism rather than his own nest. If the steady decrease in the standard of living of the upper half of Cuban society has led to the emigration of nearly one-fifth of that upper half, yet the rest have stayed to learn from the moral basis for the Revolution. Che's concept of man and his trust in man's nature have proved, on the whole, correct in Cuba. Man is not just a belly and a bank account. Society is not just a jungle. For all its external enemies and its isolation and its economic errors, the Cuban Revolution has not collapsed. And it would have foundered long ago, if Che's ideals had not prevailed over the views of the orthodox Communists, the realists and the pragmatists who tried to warp the originality of the Cuban Revolution to the tired mould of the Soviet experience. Che may have brought the Cuban economy to the edge of ruin. But apart from Fidel, no other man has brought the Cuban people to the edge of a new society in a new world. In every Cuban classroom now, the children chant, 'We will be like Che.'

6 In Search of Liberation

The life of a guerrilla fighter makes all other lives unsatisfactory. Just as Tom in *The Great Gatsby* was always seeking the dramatic turbulence of some irrecoverable football game, so Che sat behind his desk, always seeking for the irrecoverable days of the Sierra Maestra. In war, Che found his kind of peace. In liberating others, he liberated himself.

From 1960 onwards, Che had often served as a roving ambassador for Fidel Castro; he had been on important missions to Moscow—largely unsuccessful—to North Vietnam, and to other Communist and non-aligned countries. But when Che left Cuba in 1965 to become a permanent wandering fighter round the world, he was acting out his creed that the duty of the Cuban Revolution was to help other countries to fight against imperialism. And there were other reasons. Che's relationship with Fidel, while comradely and admiring, was a difficult one. The Cuban Revolution totally engaged Fidel, while Che remained preoccupied with extending the war to Latin America and to the whole world. Fidel could be a permanent revolutionary within the Cuban Revolution, Che could only be a permanent revolutionary outside it. Fidel was the leader in Cuba, Che wanted to be the leader elsewhere. Fidel had won the Cuban Revolution, Che wanted to win another revolution. Fidel was a natural and brilliant politician, Che was a natural and brilliant crusader. Fidel found satisfaction in national planning and diplomacy and speech-making, Che was bored by deals and words alone. Moreover, Fidel had found out that Che's economic ideas did not work immediately, and Che did not like a sense of failure. In the autumn of 1964, Che told Fidel that he wanted to go away to start the liberation of Latin America from the central point of Bolivia. Fidel tried to dissuade him, then began to help him to plan the new guerrilla insurrection.

Che was not the only one of the fighters from the Sierra Maestra who wanted to fight again. As Oniria Gutiérrez, a member of Che's column, recalls, 'There were some among us who always used to say that, once we had won against Batista, we would have to go and fight in other countries.' Moreover, the idea of the continuing fight against imperialism was an ideal shared by all the guerrilla leaders. As Che wrote in his farewell letter to Fidel, 'Other nations are calling for the aid of my modest efforts. I can do what you are unable to do because of your responsibility as Cuban leader.' This statement almost made Che seem to be commiserating with Fidel because Fidel could not do what both felt ought to be done.

Yet Che was a middle-aged asthmatic man, softened by years of administration, when he decided to return to active combat. Except for Garibaldi and Zapata, few revolutionary leaders have left power to go out and fight again. Like Garibaldi and Zapata, Che went out to fight again and fail. And like the other two leaders, his doomed action turned him into a folk hero of his time.

There was more good sense, however, than romanticism or boredom in Che's decision. He had an immense prestige; his presence in the field was worth a regiment. The world revolutionary movement was a daily sight in Cuba, which was crawling with schools for guerrilla training, political exiles, congresses for insurrection. The whole country was being run on something like a war footing by men in guerrilla uniform; the national mood was a state of siege. Che was merely the most important man among many who felt impelled to return to the field of combat. Some thousand Cubans have been killed in the last ten years while engaged on revolutions abroad. Seventeen Cubans went to Bolivia with Che, some of them veterans from the Sierra Maestra days. Of the seventeen, four were *comandantes*, the highest rank in the Cuban army; four were also members of the Central Committee of the Cuban Communist Party, the most responsible political positions in the island; two were over forty years old, one was a Vice Minister, one Director of Mines. In a nation which sent out its chief executives to fight in the jungles, Che's example was not unique. The Bolivian rebellion was a risk worth taking for a small island that felt itself isolated in its hemisphere. Cuba needed one, two, or three Cubas nearby.

Che also had a personal reason for going. He was an Argentine, and, however much he could protest that he felt at home anywhere, Argentina was still capitalist and unreformed. With Che's blessing, a fellow Argentine called Masetti had left in 1963 with thirty men—some of them Cubans—to initiate the liberation of Argentina from the jungles in the North. After ten months of futile floundering and growing hysteria, Masetti's force had been decimated and dispersed by the Argentine army. This debacle had affected Che, who had hoped that Masetti would prepare the way for his later coming. In fact, Masetti had called himself by the *nom de guerre* of Major Segundo, the second-in-command. Che felt that he had to avenge Masetti's failure, although he was not responsible for it, any more than Fidel was to be responsible for Che's own failure in Bolivia. It is impossible to give decisive support to an isolated guerrilla force in its early stages. The force is completely on its own and its survival is its own business.

It was also time for Che to leave Cuba. He had to take the responsibility for the failure of the early Cuban economic policy. The Russians and other East Europeans who were underwriting the Cuban economy were finding this a heavy drain on their own economies and were putting pressure on Fidel to put his house in order. The Russians wanted the Cubans to go back to supplying sugar in exchange for

Russian goods and credit, and to encourage material incentives in industry. Che could never accept such policies, so he chose to go on his travels again. In her final reply to her son, Che's mother shed a great deal of light on what Che must have hinted in his last letter to her. 'If all roads in Cuba have been closed to you, for whatever reason, in Algiers there's a Mr. Ben Bella who would appreciate your organizing his economy or advising him on it; or a Mr. Nkrumah in Ghana who would welcome the same help. Yes, you'll always be a foreigner. That seems to be your permanent fate.' Che had to move on.

Everything conspired to send Che to war a second time. In 1963, he had told *El Moujahid*, an organ of the Algerian government, that the Latin American revolution was his favourite theme. Efficient and direct himself, he could not stand the inefficiency and complexity of Cuban bureaucracy any longer. As he wrote in 1964 about a government commission, 'Since it is a commission, and since it is a government commission, it will surely dawdle and accomplish nothing.' He was certainly nostalgic for the simpler actions and plain results of guerrilla fighting. In his farewell letter to Fidel, he wrote of leaving Cuba 'with mixed feelings of joy and sorrow,' and he referred to his disillusion with administration in the ambiguous phrase, 'I leave behind the purest of my hopes as a builder.' Above all, Che felt himself a crusader in a holy war, and that was the fundamental motive for his going. As he wrote finally to Fidel, he had to fulfil 'the most sacred of duties: to fight against imperialism wherever it may be.' And this he did.

When Fidel came to speak a eulogy on Che after his death, he stated: 'In the future, high above any other, will be Che's example. National flags, prejudices, chauvinism and egoism had disappeared from his mind and heart.' This had not been true, however, between 1959 and 1964, when Che had been the faithful servant of the Cuban state, serving as an ambassador and defending Cuban policy wherever he went. Che had faithfully followed the Cuban line in international diplomacy, as it passed from psychological warfare with the United States to the encouragement of guerrilla movements in Latin America to a love affair with the Communist countries. In these six years, the expatriate and the internationalist Che seemed to have submerged himself in his honorary Cuban nationality.

By 1964, however, Che had rediscovered his old commitment to the poor nations of the world, if he had ever lost it. He began to consider that the real contradiction was not between capitalism and communism, but between developed and underdeveloped countries. Disappointment with the terms exacted by Russia and Eastern Europe for their aid to Cuba turned Che towards the concept of a Third World, made up of the poor nations from three continents, Africa and Asia and Latin America. Two other worlds opposed this Third World, a Western world and an Eastern world. Both of these two worlds consisted of powerful blocs of developed countries with high standards of living, even if they claimed to be political foes. Underdevelopment and hunger drew a different geography than did capitalism and communism. The new line divided the haves from the have-nots, the manufacturers of goods from the suppliers of raw materials, the white-skinned peoples from the dark-skinned, the colonial powers from their old possessions. The line did not clearly divide one country from another in every case; but each drawing of the line defined more clearly a Third World set apart from a Western and an Eastern power bloc.

Che's concept of a Third World has captured the popular imagination as completely as the concepts of the Yellow Peril or Manifest Destiny did in their time. This concept has led to ways of thought, even to diplomatic groupings. And that was Che's intention, as he set it out in a speech to the United Nations' Conference on Trade and Development in

March, 1964. The poor nations must not squabble for loans from the rich nations. They must show solidarity.

> *If the groups of underdeveloped countries, lured by the siren song of the vested interests of the developed powers which exploit their backwardness, contend futilely among themselves for the crumbs from the table of the world's mighty and break the ranks of numerically superior forces . . . the world will remain as it is.*

The poor nations had to learn not to undercut each other in the supplying of raw materials, nor to take bribes for joining either the Eastern or the Western bloc. Che was preaching almost the virtues of a labour union to the poor nations. In union lay strength and bargaining power; a scab nation was a villain. And his words had particular meaning for those peoples who saw themselves as Frantz Fanon's 'wretched of the earth' from the Third World, rather than as the 'wretched' hymned in the Internationale, the poor workers of the industrial nations.

In a speech to the General Assembly of the United Nations in December, 1964, Che took a more aggressive stance. He hinted that he was losing faith in peaceful solutions involving pacts, trade agreements, negotiations and foreign aid. These would not resolve the conflict between the poor and the rich. He declared, 'As Marxists we have maintained that peaceful coexistence among nations does not include coexistence between the exploiters and the exploited, the oppressor and the oppressed.' This sentence was an explicit attack on the new Russian attempt to achieve 'peaceful coexistence' with the United States, after Kennedy had made Kruschev back down and withdraw his missiles from Cuba. It was also something of a declaration of open war on imperialism.

In the same speech, Che spoke for a long time about events in the Congo since the murder of Lumumba. He revealed his own sense of personal commitment in that area.

'The free men of the world must be prepared to avenge the crime committed in the Congo.' He also revealed his new sense of identification with the non-white peoples of the world, by denouncing the white races as violently as any African nationalist.

The scales have fallen from our eyes and they now open upon new horizons, and we can see what yesterday, in our conditions of colonial servitude, we could not observe—that 'Western civilization' disguises under its showy front a scene of hyenas and jackals. That is the only name that can be applied to those who have gone to fulfil 'humanitarian' tasks in the Congo. Bloodthirsty butchers who feed on helpless people! That is what imperialism does to men; that is what marks the 'white' imperialists.

The hysteria in this passage is unlike Che's usual measured and noble sentences. It provides a clue to his state of mind at the time and to the motives for his future actions. In the light of such passion, his decision to fight in the Congo becomes understandable. Disappointed in his hopes as a 'builder' in Cuba, disgusted by the selfish and grudging help given to the underdeveloped countries by the white-skinned Communist powers of Europe, Che sloughed off his years as an administrator and Cuban diplomat, to be born again as the restless and wandering revolutionary of his youth, ready to live and feel again the sufferings of the poorest of mankind. For he had met, face to face, the wretched of the earth.

Che developed his new theme even more strongly at the Afro-Asian Solidarity Conference at Algiers in February, 1965. He now attacked Russian policy frontally, embarrassing the Cuban government and infuriating the Russians, who felt that they had already done too much for Cuba without having to be insulted as well. But they, too, had to learn that there is no gratitude in foreign aid. 'The Socialist countries,' Che declared, 'have the moral duty to liquidate their tacit complicity with the exploiting nations of the West.' To Che, there was no other valid definition of socialism than the abolition of men's exploitation of men. No country could build socialism without helping all countries to build socialism and to attack imperialism.

There are no frontiers in this struggle to the death. We cannot remain indifferent in the face of what occurs in any part of the world. A victory for any one country against imperialism is our victory, just as a defeat for any one country is a defeat for all. The practice of proletarian internationalism is not only a duty of the countries which are struggling to ensure a better future; it is also an unavoidable necessity.

Che always tried to practice what he preached. His triumph and tragedy was to commit himself out of his own mouth. This was his last call to action before taking action himself. Although the next eighteen months of his life remain obscure, it is certain that he returned to Cuba, before leaving again to fight in the Congo against the white mercenaries who had provoked his anger. Before he left Cuba, he sent the farewell message to Fidel which has been mentioned already. In it, he stated that he would try to stay true to his beliefs, whatever the final consequences; he also wrote that he had always identified with the world outcome of the Cuban Revolution. He took with him to the Congo several of his comrades from the Sierra Maestra. some of whom were to go on with him to Bolivia.

What happened to Che in the Congo is still unknown. It is likely that he joined the armed contingents of Mulele and Soumaliot in the fight against Tshombe. He and the other Cubans tried to train the Congolese to fight a guerrilla war, and they found their recruits poor material. After some nine months of relative failure, Che and his Cuban comrades decided to leave. They could not teach their African pupils anything much from their Cuban experience. A report also states that Che was sickened by something else. He found that the white mercenaries were not the only hyenas and jackals. His own side also contained butchers and cannibals. The doctor in Che was revolted.

At the time that Che was preparing to leave the Congo, a Bolivian guerrilla fighter named Coco Peredo was buying a farm on the Nancahuasu River in southern Bolivia to serve as a base for a rising against the Bolivian government of General Barrientos. The head of the Bolivian Communist Party, Mario Monje, had discussed with Fidel Castro plans to make this area the focus for a continental revolution in Latin America although it had been a military zone for thirty years. While Che returned secretly to Cuba in the autumn of 1966, various members of the guerrilla force were filtering into the country, and arms and supplies were being stockpiled in Santa Cruz and La Paz. Che himself left for Bolivia at the end of October to begin a war that he hoped would liberate the whole of his continent from the rule of imperialism. He wanted to be the new Bolívar and to be even more successful than the Great Liberator had been. Not only would he expel the power of imperialism, but he would also unite Latin America in a socialist bloc.

While he was still preparing his last rebellion, Che sent back to Cuba a message, which was read out to the Tricontinental Solidarity Organization in Havana in April, 1967. In it, Che delivered his credo before his death, his summary of philosophy gained by spending a lifetime in fighting for the poor peoples of the earth.

Che began by asking if there really had been twenty-one years of relative peace after the end of the Second World War. The war in Vietnam, for instance, had been continuing for nearly thirty years, while the people there had fought three imperialist powers in turn—Japan, France and the United States. The Vietnamese were still suffering under the bombing and escalation of the war by the Americans, who were guilty of aggression. But this guilt also applied to those, 'who, when the time came for definition, hesitated to make Vietnam an inviolable part of the socialist world; running, of course, the risks of war on a global scale—but also forcing a decision upon imperialism.' Without naming Russia or China directly, Che continued to accuse the two Communist superpowers of quarrelling with each other and of splitting the anti-imperialist forces of the world. Only the heroism of the Vietnamese in fighting for themselves had dropped the 'Great Society' of the United States into a cesspool and had convinced the North Americans that murder was no longer a good business for monopolies.

What could the Third World countries do, then, if the threat of an atomic world war caused a stalemate between the advanced communist and capitalist countries, and permitted the genocide of Vietnam? Che's answer was that the threat should be ignored. 'Since imperialists blackmail humanity by threatening it with war, the wise reaction is not to fear war.' Latin America, Africa and Asia must liberate themselves at any price. In Asia and Africa, a continental revolution was delayed; but in Latin America, it had already begun from its focal points in the guerrilla groups operating in Guatemala, Colombia, Venezuela, Peru and Bolivia. Yet if these focal points were to become real battlegrounds, then the United States would be forced to intervene with modern weapons and to commit its regular troops. This was the way to help the Vietnamese struggle and to humble the United States.

> It is the road of Vietnam; it is the road that should be followed by the people; it is the road that will be followed in Our America ... The Cuban Revolution will today have the job of ... creating a Second or a Third Vietnam, or the Second and the Third Vietnam of the world.

As imperialism was a world system, it could only be defeated by a global confrontation, a world-wide attack on the chief capitalist power, the United States. Vietnam had proved that the armed forces of the United States were vulnerable on the home ground of guerrillas fighting for their own country. A fierce ideology could beat the most advanced technology. Morale was the weak point of the North Americans, who were otherwise formidable fighters. Battles would be bloody against them and useless sacrifices should be avoided, but only fighting could defeat the economic imperialism of the United States.

> *These battles shall not be mere street fights with stones against tear-gas bombs, or pacific general strikes; neither shall it be the battle of a furious people destroying in two or three days the repressive scaffolds of the ruling oligarchies; the struggle shall be long and harsh, and its front shall be in the guerrillas' hide-out, in the cities, in the homes of the fighters . . . in the massacred rural population, in the villages and cities destroyed by the bombardments of the enemy.*
>
> *They are pushing us into this struggle; there is no alternative; we must prepare it and we must decide to undertake it.*

The beginnings of the struggle were bound to be hard. But the only way to help Vietnam was to wage total war on the North Americans. No Yankee soldier should feel safe in his quarters, in the cinema, on the town. He had to be made to feel like a cornered beast, and, as he behaved more and more like a beast, so his decadence would provoke his own downfall. All must fight together in true proletarian internationalism. To die under the flag of Vietnam or Venezuela or Guinea or Bolivia would be 'equally glorious and desirable for an American, an Asian, an African or even a European.' By fighting and dying to liberate another's country, each man was helping to liberate his own. The time for controversy between Third World groups was over. All had to combine to fight against the common imperialist enemy, the United States, which was itself beginning to break up internally in a class and race war.

> *Wherever death may surprise us, let it be welcome, provided that this, our battle-cry, may have reached some receptive ear, and another hand may be extended to wield our weapons, and other men be ready to intone the funeral dirge with the staccato chant of the machine-gun and new battle-cries of war and victory.*

So Che went to fight and die in Bolivia.

7 Death and Influence

The *Bolivian Diary* of Che Guevara is his most immediate and human statement. Scribbled each day for eleven months during an impossible struggle for survival against jungle and mountain and isolation and a trained enemy, the diary shows no dwindling towards defeat. It reveals the bare, forked, unaccommodated Che. The rhetoric is gone, the nobility, the jargon, the dialectic. There remains only the record of a great man, trying to keep his men moving and fighting as he advances towards his own death. Like another masterpiece, *Robinson Crusoe*, it is full of the catalogues of survival, the details of weapons and food and distances and supplies. The hardship and endurance, the courage and the comradeship go unsaid. They live in the spaces between the lines.

> *March 15, 1967*
> *Only we, the centre party, crossed the river, with the help of el Rubio and the Doctor. We wanted to get to the mouth of the Nancahuasu River, but three of the men cannot swim and we are heavily laden. The current carried us along nearly a kilometre, and the raft could not be used as we intended. Eleven of us stayed on this side and tomorrow the Doctor and el Rubio will cross again. We shot four hawks for our meal; they were not as bad as might be imagined. Everything has got soaked, and the weather continues to be very wet. The men's morale is low; Miguel has swollen feet and some of the others suffer from the same condition.*
> *Height—580 metres.*

So the account of a random and average day for the

guerrillas, with only an occasional death or ambush to vary the hard monotony. A recorded emotion is as rare as a victory against the enemy regiments surrounding the thirty guerrillas. When Tuma or other comrades from the old Sierra Maestra days are killed, Che sets down the loss with a brevity that is unbearably moving.

> With Tuma I lost an inseparable comrade in all the preceding years; he was loyal to the last, and I shall feel his absence from now onwards, almost as if I had lost a son. When he fell, he asked them to give me his watch . . . I will wear it throughout the war. We put the body on an animal and took it away to bury far from there.

Heroic tragedy demands a sense of inevitable fate. Throughout the *Bolivian Diary*, the presence of death broods. Che did not go to fight in Bolivia to get himself killed; but he knew that the odds were against his survival. After all, the beginning of the Cuban campaign had taught him that the whole group could easily be wiped out in the opening stages, as had nearly happened at Alegría de Pío. Luck had to aid the guerrilla group as well as skill at keeping alive. And luck ran out for Che in Bolivia.

Because Che was killed and because the Bolivian insurrection failed initially, it is easy to be wise after the event. There were many factors which made a success in Bolivia more unlikely than in Cuba. First, Che and the other guerrilla leaders were Cubans, while revolution in Latin America has always had a strong nationalistic streak. There was friction within the guerrilla group itself between the Cuban and the Bolivian comrades, while the Bolivian Indians not only distrusted the Cubans as foreigners, but also as another lot of lying white men. Secondly, Bolivia had had a land reform during its previous left-wing régime. The Bolivian Indians might be miserably poor, but they did own their own barren soil for the first time in three hundred years, and an acre in the hand was worth any utopia in the bush. Che's total failure to recruit one single peasant to the guerrilla cause during his eleven months of preparation and fighting was the basic cause of his defeat. As Che had stated in his own book, *Guerrilla Warfare*, the fundamental reason for the success in Cuba had been the aid of the peasants in the Sierra Maestra. 'To try and carry out this kind of war without the support of the population is the prelude to inevitable disaster.'

Other factors doomed the guerrillas. Isolation was the worst blow. The middle-class sympathizers in the large cities were soon betrayed by a couple of the weaker guerrillas, who defected. Parallel risings in Peru and other Latin American countries fizzled out, through a failure of nerve and communications. Because Che could not bring himself to be ruthless enough to kill potential traitors both inside and outside of the guerrilla force, first his base camp fell into enemy hands with the loss of vital asthma medicines and supplies and papers, then his own small force split up into two parts that were hunted down and destroyed separately. A certain resignation and lack of aggression in Che as a commander also began to show itself, as he grew physically sick and weak. Once he even became hysterical enough to stab a faithful mare. His heroism lay in his unceasing struggle against the sight of his group's and his own decomposition. As long as he could stand, he would fight on.

Internal political factors in Bolivia helped Che's defeat. General Barrientos was, after all, a Bolivian. And although Che could rightly accuse him of accepting North American arms and advisers, Barrientos could accuse the guerrillas with justice of being wholly led and supplied by Cuban Communists. Fidel had refused to take many non-Cubans on the *Granma*, for fear that his rebellion should be thought to be a foreign invasion; Che was not so wise. Moreover, Che's greatest failure lay in his lack of suppleness as a politician. He had to compromise with one man, Mario

Monje, to end his isolation and to stop his group being strangled by vastly superior forces. Monje was the head of the Bolivian Communist Party, and Che had to have his help in fomenting unrest in the mines and in La Paz. Fidel in Cuba had been frankly shifty about the pledges he gave to urban politicians to get their support; Che coolly dismissed Fidel's later reneging on his promises with the words :

We were not satisfied with this compromise, but it was necessary; at that time, it was progressive. It could not last beyond the time when it became a brake on revolutionary development, but we were willing to go along with it.

But Che would not compromise with Monje. When Monje demanded that the Bolivian Communist Party lead the insurrection as the price of its support, Che stated that he had to be the chief. In fact, he would have been the chief in practice, fighting in isolation in the jungles and mountains; but he had to be the theoretical chief as well. That was the Cuban creed; the actual guerrillas should lead. Monje had, anyway, betrayed his promises to Fidel that the Bolivian Communist Party would back Che on any terms. Che was the field commander; he had to lead, by his own theory. Che would rather die than deny himself.

Yet, despite these difficulties and errors, the Bolivian insurrection could have overthrown the Barrientos government, and it still fights on. The original theory of the Cuban Revolution, that the revolution makes itself and that conditions are never good enough for rational men to start a revolution, nearly received a second startling confirmation. After the jaunty rebel attack on Sumaipata in July, 1967, when a few guerrillas captured a whole town and its garrison, the Barrientos government tottered with the laughter of the people. The legend of the guerrillas led by Che caused both Argentina and Peru to close their frontiers and to mobilize troops. Bolivia was, apparently, becoming the

focus for a continental revolution, particularly as there had
been a spontaneous rising in June in the Bolivian mines,
which the army had suppressed with great brutality. Had
Che been more aggressive at this moment and attacked
with his twenty-two men the defenceless oilfields and communications of Bolivia, the growing legend of the invincible
guerrillas would have brought in recruits and might well
have caused the downfall of Barrientos, who had many
enemies waiting to capitalize on popular discontent. But
Che was too cautious, the quality of the Bolivian army's
strategy began to improve, and the handful of guerrillas
began to fall into the sort of ambushes they had been so
clever in setting. During the last three months of his guerrilla campaign, Che was on the run and losing.

Even the disaster at the Yuro Ravine, when the wounded
Che was himself captured and his group dispersed, was
hardly worse than the disaster at Alegría de Pío. Ten men
survived the debacle, although five of these were later
rounded up by the Bolivian army. Of the others, three of
the Cubans reached safety in Chile, and the leading Bolivian
guerrilla, Inti Peredo, turned back into Bolivia to continue
the struggle, which is still being fought. In 1968, Inti Peredo
sent out a dispatch from Bolivia, which stated:

> *Guerrilla warfare in Bolivia is not dead! It has just*
> *begin ... The irreparable physical death of our friend*
> *and comrade, our Major Ernesto Che Guevara, as well as*
> *of many other fighters, has been a rude blow to us ... But*
> *these painful events, far from frightening us, strengthen*
> *our revolutionary awareness ...*
>
> *Our single and final goal is the liberation of Latin*
> *America, which is more than a continent; it is rather our*
> *homeland, temporarily torn into twenty republics.*
>
> *We are convinced that the dream of Bolívar and Che—*
> *that of uniting Latin America both politically and geo-*
> *graphically—will be attained through armed struggle,*

which is the only dignified, honest, glorious and irreversible method which will motivate the people.

The care that the Bolivian army authorities took to assassinate the wounded Che and to burn his body and to scatter his ashes showed the fear that the military governments of Latin America felt about Che's legend and Che's dream of uniting the continent through armed struggle. They knew that his cause would not die with his body. They might make cinders of his corpse, but they could not make cinders of his ideal. Pombo, who had been Che's bodyguard and who escaped from Bolivia back to Cuba, refuses to admit the failure of the Bolivian attempt. 'It didn't fail,' he says. 'We lost a battle.' And he continues, 'The guerrilla group, like men, is at birth an almost defenceless creature, a child. If ours had survived, he would have grown and developed. But in Bolivia there was one failure: they discovered us too early and we had to fight.' The ideal of an armed continental revolution spreading from a guerrilla focus near the centre of the continent is not dead among the followers of Che. It is postponed until the next rising.

In death, Che has had more influence than when he was alive. Dead men may tell no tales, but they can make a legend. Che was not only one of the more heroic men of his age; he was also one of the more intelligent, more original, more ascetic, more radical, more human and more beautiful men of his age. His face has launched a thousand turmoils, his words a hundred revolts. He has provided the Marxists with a kind of saint, who has dedicated his life and death to the poorest of men without help from God. The walls of the student halls of the world are chalked with the words, CHE LIVES. His martyrdom has been the condition for his inspiration of the young. He may have died for the poor, but he also died for the future.

More immediately, Che's death coincided with the full

fury of the Red Guard movement in Mao's China. With Che as their personal symbol and the Red Guards as their general model, many of the students of the world revolted in 1968. The events of 1968 were curiously similar to those of 1848, when a wave of insurrection swept through most of the capital cities of Europe and ended in the victory of the powers that were. The chief difference between the student revolts of 1968 and the middle-class revolts of 1848 lay in the form of the new inspiration. For both Che and the Red Guards were inspired by the concept of a rural revolt that would sweep up out of the countryside to purge the corruption of the cities. The middle-class students who fought in the streets of Paris during the May Revolution, or of Chicago during the Democratic Convention, or of Berlin or London or Buenos Aires or Tokyo or Mexico City or twenty other cities during the year after Che's death came from an urban or suburban setting. They did not want to know of their misconception of Che's and Mao's thought. Yet Mao was to remind them, when he sent twenty million of the Red Guards back to labour in the country-side. As the *New China Daily* told the parents of Chinese youth, 'The greatest love one can give one's sons and daughters is to encourage them to go to the front line of production and to temper themselves in the countryside . . . through re-education by the poor peasants.'

The governments of the world won in 1968. In Latin America, nearly all the guerrilla risings were suppressed. In Communist and capitalist countries, in developed and in underdeveloped countries, the protest of the young was defeated by the power of the old. Harsher measures were taken in Kenya as well as in Czechoslovakia, in Mexico as well as in France, in China as well as in the United States. It was a global reaction against a global revolt partially inspired by Che's death. But just as Bolívar failed five times before succeeding in Latin America, and Che himself failed three times in Guatemala and the Congo and Bolivia for his

89

one success in Cuba, so the failure of the revolts of 1968 did not mean the end of revolts. For Che's most explosive idea was that the revolution is permanent and that the revolution creates itself. Authority has not sat safe in its seats since that heresy reached the minds of the young.

The reasons for the cult of Che Guevara are both personal and cultural. In himself, he came from a bourgeois, white, prosperous, educated, suburban background, as do so many of the new middle-class student revolutionary leaders of our time, who despair at the capacity of the old-style Communist Parties and labour unions to lead any sort of revolution at all. These new radicals find it easy to identify with Che. What he did and tried to do makes the impossible for them possible. He was not a product of historical necessity. He was a revolutionary who chose to be so. Thus his example gives hope to all those, such as Régis Debray, who wish to work for the poor and the lost of the world without having been born black or oppressed or underprivileged. Birth did not make Che. He was self-made.

While the revolutionary remains the hero of our times, no other revolutionary hero will supplant Che. The rapid development of his cult after his death was the logical outcome of the end of his life, which was already spent in the whisper of secrecy, mystery, potency and combat. Che's cowardly murder brought him instant consecration, because his death made certain all the qualities ascribed to him. His choice to leave Cuba and his martyrdom for his cause set him above Fidel Castro or Ho Chi Minh or Mao Tse-Tung as a symbol of revolution, even if his talents as a guerrilla leader may have been inferior. If Che had remained in Cuba or had died accidentally like Camilo Cienfuegos, his portrait would not be paraded by students all over the world, his example would not be quoted everywhere, his works would not be so widely read. Not only Marxists, but almost all progressives, and even pacifists who qualify their admiration for Che by warning that they disagree with some of his methods, would agree with Fidel's praise of Che's qualities as a man : 'If we wish to express what we want the men of future generations to be, we must say : "Let them be like Che!"'

In every cult there is an element of the untrue and the irrational. In the cult of Che, that element is his identification with Christ. Because he fought for the poor and because he chose to be sacrificed in his prime, he gives a mystical feeling that he died for *us*, for all humanity. Clearly, he killed other men. Clearly, he hated his enemies. Clearly, his beliefs stemmed from political doctrines loathsome to many. Clearly, he advocated and used tactics that were sometimes dubious or inhuman. Clearly, he was a man who lived in his muck and sweat like a beast in the jungle. Yet clearly, he transcends all these facts. He appears as larger than a human being, as somebody approaching a saviour. When all is said and done, when his words and acts have been coldly seen and sometimes condemned, the conviction remains that Che was always driven by his love for humanity and for the good in mankind. The ideals expressed in his writings, his whole life and his passion and his death, transcend ideology. The photograph of his corpse now is pinned as an eikon in many country homes across Catholic Latin America.

Sartre was correct when he called Che 'the most complete man of his age.' There was a Renaissance quality about Che; he had more careers in thirty-nine years than a whole squad of men have in their lives, and he had more lives than any litter of cats. He tried to be professional in everything he did, as a doctor, a diarist, a political and military theorist, a guerrilla fighter, an economist, a tactician, a banker, a planner, an industrialist, an ambassador, a propagandist and as the doer of all his other duties. But he was complete in more than his work. He was all of a piece. He seems to have had hardly any contradictions or inner conflicts. He was amazingly consistent in all he said and thought and did. The professional administrator who discussed the economy of Latin America was no different from the guerrilla hero in Bolivia, who had decided that combat was the only way of solving his continent's social and economic problems. The difference between Che and other men was that Che did not let other men put his ideas into practice. He practised them himself.

There was no duality between Che's actions and his words. The writer practised what he preached, and put other intellectuals to shame. The man of action set down his experiences and analysed them to draw practical and moral conclusions from them. The dreamer applied his skills in trying to make his dreams concrete. Che was an absolutist. He wanted to pursue everything to its just conclusion. His consistency was almost maddening in its effortlessness. There was no trace of hypocrisy in him. When he said that working for one's fellow men was the greatest joy a man could have, it was true for him. He thought it was fit for a revolutionary to go and die under the flag of a nation not yet born, and he did just that, not making a great display of courage, but being courageous and cheerful as if he were doing the most natural thing in all the world. He said that no one was irreplacable and really felt that this applied to him as much as to anyone else. So he exposed himself and died. He was a complete man.

History will probably treat Guevara as the Garibaldi of his age, the most admired and loved revolutionary of his time. The impact of his ideas on socialism and guerrilla warfare may be temporary; but his influence, particularly in Latin America, must be lasting. For there has been no man with so great an ideal of unity for that divided and unlucky continent since Bolívar. The young will find new heroes, but none more inspiring. And the consequences of his death are only beginning to be seen in the social upheavals and changes around us. When the general in *Viva Zapata* looks down at the riddled corpse of the dead guerrilla leader, he says, 'Sometimes a dead man can be a terrible enemy.' For the rich nations of the earth, and for the corrupt governments that rule many of the poor nations, the dead Che is a terrible and a beautiful enemy.

Further Reading

Ernesto 'Che' Guevara, *Reminiscences of the Cuban Revolutionary War* (Allen & Unwin), *Guerrilla Warfare* (Cassell), *Venceremos: Speeches and Writings* (J. Gerassi ed., Wiedenfeld & Nicolson), *Bolivian Diary* (Cape/Lorrimer)

Régis Debray, *Revolution in the Revolution?* (Pelican)

Fidel Castro and Régis Debray, *On Trial* (Lorrimer)

Ricardo Rojo, *My Friend Che* (Dial)

Fidel Castro and others, *Viva Che* (Lorrimer)

Carlos Franqui, *Cuba: Le Livre des Douze* (Gallimard)

Herbert Matthews, *Castro: A Political Biography* (Penguin)

For permission to quote from works in copyright, including some re-translation by the author, acknowledgement is due to the following: to Messrs. George Allen and Unwin, Ltd., London, and Monthly Review Press, Inc., New York (Copyright © 1968 by Monthly Review Press, Inc.) for extracts from *Reminiscences of the Cuban Revolutionary War* by Che Guevara; to Dial Press, Inc., New York, for extracts from *My Friend Che*, by Ricardo Rojo; to Weidenfeld (Publishers) Ltd., London, for extracts from *Venceremos: Speeches and Writings*, edited by J. Gerassi.

Fontana Modern Masters

Edited by Frank Kermode

Marcuse

Alasdair MacIntyre

Until a few years ago, Herbert Marcuse's reputation was confined to academic circles. Recently his analysis of the predicament of man in modern industrial society has been a source of revolutionary ideas and slogans. Is Marcuse's analysis soundly based? Are his conclusions true? These are the questions that Alasdair MacIntyre pursues through an examination of the content, method, and conclusions of Marcuse's thought, and his relationship to other writers, notably Hegel, Freud and Marx. The answers he gives are forthright, closely argued, and highly critical.

Camus

Conor Cruise O'Brien

In this book Conor Cruise O'Brien reinterprets Camus as a writer who, more than any other, represents the Western consciousness, and conscience, in its relation to the non-Western world. In a close and brilliant analysis of Camus's work Dr. O'Brien discerns a tension between Europe and Africa, submerged in the early works but coming more and more into the open; and he portrays Camus's life as a great personal tragedy, a defeat for a generation.

Fontana Modern Masters

Edited by Frank Kermode

Fanon
David Caute

Frantz Fanon is known as a champion of Africa against Europe, of black against white: 'Every brother on a rooftop can quote Fanon', it was said in the Chicago riots of 1967. But Fanon transcended race war, as David Caute brings out in this moving and sympathetic study. He was a defender of the poor against the power elites, whether white or black; and his ideal for a Third World liberated from the West was for all mankind: 'Let us try to create the whole man, whom Europe has been incapable of bringing to triumphant birth.'

Lévi-Strauss
Edmund Leach

The theories of Claude Lévi-Strauss aim at no less than an understanding of the human mind. They combine, to quote the author of this book, 'baffling complexity' with 'overwhelming erudition'. In unravelling the complexities, Dr. Leach balances a sharply critical approach to his subject with a generous recognition of its importance, and he combines erudition with consideration for the layman.